OPEN LETTER

— TO —

CONFUSED CATHOLICS

by His Excellency
Archbishop Marcel Lefebvre

Translated from the French

ANGELUS PRESS
2915 FOREST AVENUE,
KANSAS CITY, MISSOURI 64109

Library of Congress Cataloging-in-Publication Data

Lefebvre, Marcel, 1905-
[Lettre ouverte aux catholiques perplexes. English]
Open Letter to confused Catholics / by His Excellency Archbishop Marcel Lefebvre ;
translated from the French.
163p.; 22cm.
ISBN 0-935952-13-6
Includes bibliographical references
1. Catholic Church--Controversial literature. 2. Catholic traditionalist movement.
BX1779.5 .L4413   1986   98-119542
282.09 04 21   CIP

ANGELUS PRESS
2915 FOREST AVENUE
KANSAS CITY, MISSOURI 64109
PHONE (816) 753-3150
FAX (816) 753-3557
ORDER LINE 1-800-966-7337
www.angeluspress.org

ISBN 0-935952-13-6

First Published in France by Editions Albin Michel
First English translation by Society of Saint Pius X—Great Britain 1986

FIRST PRINTING—November 1987
SECOND PRINTING—April 1989
THIRD PRINTING—November 1992
FOURTH PRINTING—November 1995
FIFTH PRINTING—March 1999
SIXTH PRINTING—April 2001
SEVENTH PRINTING—August 2006

Printed in the United States of America

TABLE OF CONTENTS

PREFACE

While presenting in English Archbishop Lefebvre's recently published book (his only one apart from some collections of addresses), I feel there is a need also of some words of introduction to the author himself—so well known by name, but so little known as he truly is.

Beginning life in an exemplary Catholic family of the north of France, Marcel Lefebvre knew his vocation from an early age. He joined the Holy Ghost Fathers, and, after the usual training, his life was that of a missionary and seminary professor. It became recognized that he had, to an exceptional degree, the qualities of a bishop, and he was promoted to Archbishop of Dakar and eventually became Apostolic Delegate, the Pope's representative, to all of French-speaking Africa. For six years he was also Superior General of his Order, the largest of the missionary congregations.

So Archbishop Lefebvre is, first and foremost, a missionary bishop, and typical of what a bishop should be. His qualities are not showy, they are those of a Christian ruler, which is what a bishop is: reliability, straightforwardness, calmness, approachability, with the capacity for making decisions and sticking to them. Such a man would never, in ordinary times, have been controversial; he would have continued administering and inspiring day-to-day work of the missions until his eventual retirement to the position of an "elder statesman." What brought him into the limelight, and made him an object of opprobrium—or admiration—all over the Catholic world, is the revolutionary situation in the Church—it is nothing less—that has been developing since the Second Vatican Council.

There is no need for me to enlarge on that situation now: it is the subject matter of this book, the first part of which is a factual study of what is going on in the Catholic Church, while in the second part, the causes of it are examined. Here readers will also find the answers to their questions about the author's personal involvement.

The Archbishop's wide experience makes his analysis an authoritative one. His writing has also a quality that may be unexpected, for all who have only heard about him—it is so eminently reasonable. If he is a "rebel," (as we never cease being told!), he is an uncommonly calm and courteous one. If this comes as a surprise, it is because he has been given little opportunity to make himself known. He has been conveniently buried in silence, except when quoted as an example of obstinate backwardness, by all who are embarrassed by the accusations he makes, or simply the positions he adopts. In view of this, the publishing of this book is a belated act of justice.

He causes embarrassment in the manner of the little boy in Hans Christian Andersen's parable, who alone spoke the obvious truth: "The Emperor has no clothes!" Among the chorus of satisfaction at the renewal of the Church by Vatican II, the Archbishop asks what, precisely, this renewal consists in. And he points out the facts that can be shown by statistics: the dramatic decline in baptisms, confirmations and ordinations, in the numbers of monks and nuns, and of schools; not to mention the confusion among the faithful, especially the rising generation, about what Catholic belief is. In this situation, he asks first and foremost for truthfulness (which in revolutions is always one of the first casualties)—truthfulness as to the facts of the present situation, and also with regard to the established teaching of the Church. He knows that the blurring with a view to some immediate advantage is disastrous for the faith of Catholics, and unjust to the others for whose supposed benefit it is usually done. His frank acceptance of established doctrine gives the Archbishop's writing another characteristic that one is grateful for: its perfect clarity. He knows his mind because he knows what his faith is.

It is likely that some who read these pages will be alerted for the first time to the extent of the disintegration of the Catholic Church. If they are shocked into a realization that a revolution is in progress which, if it continues, will eventually engulf their parish also, they may nevertheless find some of the Archbishop's language a little exaggerated: he may seem too *absolute*. How, for example, can he calmly dismiss as unfit for Christians ideas like Liberalism, Religious Liberty and Socialism?

Here, a word of explanation is called for. We must remember that His Grace is writing against the background of France, where ideas are generally more clear-cut than they are in Great Britain, or at any rate, in England. Take the word "socialism," for example; that means to some of us, first and foremost, a social ideal of brotherhood and justice. We have had our christian socialists. On the Continent, however, Socialism is uncompromisingly anti-religious, or almost a substitute for religion, and communism is seen as the natural development from it. This is the Socialism the Archbishop is writing about. And when he rejects Liberalism, he is not thinking of the Liberal Party, or of the virtue of liberality, but of that religious liberalism that exalts human liberty above the claims of God or of His Church, and which Newman said that it had been his life's work to combat. It is because Vatican II's *Declaration on Religious Liberty* contains phrases that encourage this liberalism that the Archbishop asks for its revision. Modernism, too, has a special meaning: not a simpley urge to be up-to-date, but the particular system of ideas which was condemned by Pope St. Pius X on the grounds that, on the pretext of making Revelation acceptable to the modern mentality, it destroyed the very foundations of belief in revealed Truth. And while making these clarifications, we may mention the word "Revolution," as used by the author. Sometimes he is referring to the French Revolution of 1789, with its slogan of "Liberty, Equality, Fraternity"; but he also, especially in Chapter XV, uses the word to indicate the general revolt against the Church which made its appearance in some aspects of the Renaissance, was nurtured by the Freemasons, burst out violently in 1789, and proceeded to produce Marxist Communism. The same rejection of God and His

Revelation inspires all these phases.

A Catholic facing the evidence of disintegration presented here might well be tempted to despair. Archbishop Lefebvre does not despair because he knows that the Church, despite all appearances, is guaranteed by Our Lord Jesus Christ as being His chosen representative on earth, by which He conveys to all men the benefits of the Redemption. It is this unwavering faith that gives him what is perhaps his outstanding quality—the courage that was needed to stand firm, isolated, against the urgent pressures of those he had been taught to revere as defenders of the Faith, and who were ready to welcome him with open arms in return for some simple compromise. So exposed a position is perilous and, he has a right to expect the support of the prayers of those of us who recognize his special service to the Church: that of training priests and nuns who preserve the tried traditions that are the foundation on which an eventual, true renewal can be based.

Though responsibility for the translation is mine, it has been a team enterprise, which will have its sufficient reward in the appearance of the book. Credit for it is due first to Mr. John Noon, who broke the back of the work, and also, for different sections, to Mr. Malcolm Potter and to Father Philip M. Stark; and not least to Mrs. Ann Nott for typing the scripts for printing.

Father Michael Crowdy
1986

I
Why are Catholics Confused?

Who can deny that Catholics in the latter part of the twentieth century are confused? A glance at what has happened in the Church over the past twenty years is enough to convince anyone that this is a relatively recent phenomenon. Only a short time ago the path was clearly marked: either one followed it or one did not. One had the Faith—or perhaps had lost it—or had never had it. But he who had it—who had entered the Church through baptism, who had renewed his baptismal promises around the age of twelve and had received the Holy Ghost on the day of his confirmation—such a person knew what he had to believe and what he had to do.

Many today no longer know. They hear all sorts of astonishing statements in the churches, they read things contrary to what was always taught, and doubt has crept into their minds.

On June 30, 1968, at the close of the Year of Faith, His Holiness Pope Paul VI made a profession of the Catholic Faith, in the presence of all the bishops in Rome and hundreds of thousands of the faithful. In his introductory remarks, he put us on guard against attacks on Catholic doctrine which, he said, "give rise, as we regretfully see today, to trouble and confusion in many faithful souls."

The same words crop up in an allocution of His Holiness Pope John Paul II on February 6, 1981: "Christians today, in large part, feel lost, perplexed, confused, and even deceived." The Holy Father summarized the underlying causes of the trouble as follows:

"We see spread abroad ideas contrary to the truth
which God has revealed and which the Church has always
taught. Real heresies have appeared in dogma and moral
theology, stirring doubt, confusion, rebellion. Even the liturgy has been harmed. Christians have been plunged into
an intellectual and moral illuminism, a sociological Christianity, without clear dogma or objective morality."

This confusion is seen everywhere—in conversations, in
books, in newspapers, in radio and television broadcasts, in
the behavior of Catholics, which shows up as a sharp decline in the practice of the faith as statistics reveal, a dissatisfaction with the Mass and the sacraments, a general re-
laxation of morals.

We naturally ask, therefore, what brought on this state
of things? For every effect there is a cause. Has faith been
weakened by a disappearance of generosity of soul, by a
taste for enjoyment, an attraction to the pleasures of life and
the manifold distractions which the modern world offers?
These cannot be the real reasons, because they have always
been with us in one way or another. The rapid decline in
religious practice comes rather from the new spirit which
has been introduced into the Church and which has cast
suspicion over all past teachings and life of the Church. All
this was based on the unchangeable faith of the Church,
handed down by catechisms which were recognized by all
bishops.

The faith was based on certitudes. The certitudes have
been overturned and confusion has resulted. Let us take
one example: the Church taught—and the faithful believed—that the Catholic religion was the one true religion.
It was, in fact, established by God Himself, while other religions are the work of men. Consequently, the Christian
must avoid all contact with false religions and, furthermore,
do all he can to bring adherents of false religions to the religion of Christ.

Is this still true? Indeed it is! Truth cannot change—else
it never was the truth. No new fact, no theological or scientific discovery—if there can be such a thing as a theological

discovery—can ever make the Catholic religion any less the only means of salvation.

But now we have the Pope himself attending religious ceremonies in false religions, praying and preaching in the churches of heretical sects. Television conveys to the whole world pictures of these astonishing events. The faithful no longer understand.

Martin Luther—and I shall return to him later in these pages—cut entire nations off from the Church, pitched Europe into a spiritual and political turmoil which destroyed the Catholic hierarchy over wide areas, invented a false doctrine of salvation and a false doctrine of the sacraments. His revolt against the Church became the model for all revolutionaries after him who would throw Europe and the whole world into disorder. It is impossible to make Luther, as they want to do now after five hundred years, into a prophet or doctor of the Church, since he is not a saint.

If I read *Documentation Catholique* or the diocesan papers, I find there, from the Joint Catholic-Lutheran Commission, officially recognized by the Vatican, statements like this:

> "Among the ideas of the Second Vatican Council, we can see gathered together much of what Luther asked for, such as the following: description of the Church as 'the people of God' (a learning idea of the new Canon Law—a democatic, no longer hierarchic, idea); accent on the priesthood of all baptized; the right of the individual to freedom of religion. Other demands of Luther in his time can be considered as being met in the theology and practice of the Church today: use of the common language in the liturgy, possibility of Communion under two species, a renewal of the theology and celebration of the Eucharist."

Quite a statement! Meeting the demands of Luther, who declared himself the resolute and mortal enemy of the Mass and of the pope! To gather together things requested by a blasphemer who said: "I declare that all brothels, murders, thefts, adulteries, are less evil than this abominable Mass!" From such an extravagant summary, we can draw only one conclusion: either we must condemn the Second Vatican Council which authorized it, or we must condemn the Council of Trent and all the popes who, since the sixteenth century, have declared Protestantism heretical and schismatic.

It is understandable that Catholics are confused by such a turn of events. But there are so many others! In a few years they have seen a transformation in the heart and substance of religious practices which adults have known from early childhood. In the churches, the altars have been demolished or replaced by tables, which are often portable and disappear when not in use. The tabernacle no longer occupies the place of honor: most of the time it is hidden, perhaps perched on a post, to one side. When it remains in the center, the priest turns his back to it during the Mass. Celebrant and faithful face each other and dialogue. Anyone may touch the sacred vessels, which are often replaced by bread-baskets, platters, ceramic bowls. Laity, including women, distribute Communion, which is received in the hand. The Body of Christ is treated with a lack of reverence which casts doubt on the truth of transubstantiation.

The Sacraments are administered in a manner which varies from place to place; I will cite as examples the age for baptism and confirmation, variations in the nuptial blessing, introduction of chants and readings which have nothing to do with the liturgy, but are borrowed from other religions or a purely secular literature, sometimes simply to express political ideas.

Latin, the universal language of the Church, and Gregorian Chant have generally disappeared. All the hymns have been replaced by modern songs in which it is not uncommon to find the same rhythms as in places of entertainment.

Catholics have been surprised also by the sudden disappearance of religious garb, as if priests and religious were ashamed of looking like what they are.

Parents who send their children to catechism discover that the truths of the Faith are no longer taught, even the most basic: the Holy Trinity, the mystery of the Incarnation, Original Sin, the Immaculate Conception. Hence the feeling of profound disorientation: is all of this no longer true, out-of-date, *passe?* Christian virtues are no longer even mentioned. Where can you find a catechism speaking of humility, chastity, mortification? The Faith has become a fluid concept, charity a kind of universal solidarity, and hope is, above all, hope for a better world.

Novelties like these are not the kind which, in the human situation, appear at a certain moment in time, so that we get accustomed to them and assimilate them after an initial period of surprise and uncertainty. In the course of a human life, ways of doing things change. If I were still a missionary in Africa, I would go there by plane and no longer by boat—if, indeed, you could find a steamship company still in operation. In this sense, we can say that one should live in one's own time; one is really forced to do so.

But those Catholics on whom they tried to impose novelties in the spiritual and supernatural order, on the same principle, realized it was not possible. You do not change the Holy Sacrifice of the Mass, the Sacraments founded by Jesus Christ; you do not change the truth revealed once and for all; you do not replace one dogma with another. The pages which follow try to answer the questions you are asking yourselves; you who have known another face of the Church. I shall try also to enlighten the young people born after the Council and to whom the Catholic community does not offer what they have a right to expect from it. I would like to address myself, finally, to the unconcerned and the agnostics, whom the grace of God will touch some day or another, but who by then may find the churches without priests, and a teaching which does not correspond to the needs of their souls.

Then there is a question which, by all evidence, interests everyone, if I can judge by the attention it gets in the general press, especially in France. (The journalists are also showing some confusion.) A few headlines: "Is Christianity Dying?" "Will Time Work Against the Religion of Jesus

Christ?" "Will There Still Be Priests in the Year 2000?"
These questions I hope also to answer, not with any new
theory of my own, but relying on unbroken Catholic Tradition—unbroken, yet so neglected in recent years that to
many readers it will seem no doubt like something entirely
new.

II
"They Are Changing Our Religion!"

Firstly, I must dispel a misunderstanding so as not to have to return to it. I am not the head of a movement, even less the head of a particular church. I am not, as they never stop writing, "the leader of the traditionalists." They have come to describe certain persons as "Lefebvrists," as though it were a case of a party or a school. This is an abuse of language.

I have no personal doctrine in the matter of religion. All my life I have held to what I was taught at the French Seminary in Rome, namely Catholic doctrine according to the interpretation given it by the teaching authority of the Church from century to century, since the death of the last Apostle which marked the end of Revelation.

There should be nothing in that to feed the appetite for sensationalist journalists and, through them, current public opinion. Yet, on the 29th of August, 1976, the whole of France was excited on hearing that I was going to say Mass at Lille. What was so extraordinary about a bishop celebrating the Holy Sacrifice? I had to preach before a panoply of microphones and each of my remarks was greeted as if it were a striking declaration. Yet what did I say beyond what any other bishop could have said?

There lies the key to the enigma: the other bishops had been for a number of years no longer saying the same things. How often, for example have you heard them speaking of the social reign of Our Lord Jesus Christ?

My personal experience never ceases to amaze me. These bishops for the most part were fellow students with

me in Rome, trained in the same manner. And then, all of a
sudden, I found myself alone. But I have invented nothing
new; I was carrying on. Cardinal Garrone even said to me
one day: "They deceived us at the French Seminary in
Rome." Deceived us in what? Had he not himself taught the
children of his catechism class thousands of times, before
the Council, the Act of Faith: "My God, I firmly believe all
the truths Thou hast revealed and that Thy Church doth
teach, because Thou canst neither deceive nor be deceived."?

How have all these bishops been able to metamorphose
themselves in this manner? I can see only one explanation:
they were always in France and they let themselves become
gradually infected. In Africa I was protected. I came back
the year of the Council, when the harm had already been
done. Vatican II only opened the gates which were holding
back the devastating flood. In no time at all, even before the
end of the fourth session, it was catastrophic. Everything,
almost, was to be swept away; prayer first of all.

Any Christian who has an instinct for God, a respect for
Him, must be shocked by the manner in which prayers are
said now. Learning prayers by heart, as we did, is now
denigrated as "parrot-fashion." Children are no longer
taught the words nor do they appear now in the catechisms, except for the Our Father. And even that is in a
new version, of Protestant inspiration, which makes the
child address God as "*tu.*" To do this systematically is not
a sign of great reverence, and is foreign to the spirit of our
language, which offers us a choice of styles according to
whether we are addressing a superior or a parent or a
friend. And in the same post-conciliar Our Father, one asks
God not to "lead us into temptation," an expression that is
equivocal, at least; while our traditional French version is
an improvement upon the Latin, which is rather clumsily
based on the Hebrew. What progress is there in this? The
familiar style of speech has also invaded the whole body of
vernacular liturgy: the new Sunday Missal makes it exclusive and obligatory, though one can see no reason for a

change so contrary to French style and custom.

Tests have been made in Catholic schools with children of twelve or thirteen. Only a few knew the Our Father by heart (in French, naturally), and a few knew their Hail Mary. With one or two exceptions these children did not know the Apostles' Creed, the I Confess, the Acts of Faith, Hope, Charity and Contrition, or the Angelus or the Memorare. How could they know them, when most of them had never even heard them said? Prayer must be "spontaneous," we must speak to God out of the abundance of the heart, so they tell us now; and they scorn the marvellous educational system of the Church which has produced and perfected all these prayers, which have been the support of the greatest saints.

How many still practice and encourage morning and evening prayers together in the family, or the saying of the prayers of blessing and thanksgiving at meals? I have learned that in many Catholic schools they no longer want the prayer at the start of the lesson, on the pretext that some of the pupils are unbelievers or belong to other religions, and that it would not do to affront their consciences or display a triumphalist spirit. They congratulate themselves on receiving in these schools a large majority of non-Catholics and even non-Christians, and doing nothing to lead them to God. The young Catholics, meanwhile, must conceal their faith: this on the pretext of respecting the opinions of their schoolmates.

The genuflection is now practised only by a small number of the faithful; it has been replaced by a nod of the head, or more often by nothing at all. One enters a church and sits down. The furniture has been changed, the *prie-dieus* broken up for firewood. Often seats have been installed similiar to those in cinemas, thereby allowing the public to be more comfortably seated when the church is used for a concert. I have been told of the case of the Blessed Sacrament Chapel in a big parish church in Paris, which used to be visited by a number of people working nearby during their lunch hour. One day it was closed for work to be carried out. When the doors were opened again the *prie-dieus* had disappeared. On a comfortable pile carpet were deep upholstered seats, evidently expensive and of the sort found in the reception foyers of big companies or airlines. The comportment of the faithful changed at once: some knelt on the carpet, but most made themselves comfortable and meditated before the tabernacle cross-legged. The parish clergy certainly had some intention in their minds; one does not embark on expensive changes or alterations without thinking of what one is doing. What we are seeing here is the desire to modify the relationship of man to God in the direction of familiarity and casualness, as if we were dealing with Him as equals. How can one acquire a conviction that one is in the presence of the Creator and Sovereign Lord of all things, if one suppresses the gestures that embody the "virtue of Religion"? Does one not also run the risk of diminishing the sense of the Real Presence in the tabernacle?

Catholics are likewise bewildered by the obstinate partiality to banality and even vulgarity, in the manner in which places of worship are treated. Everything that contributed to the beauty of the buildings and the splendor of the ceremonies is decried as "triumphalism." The *décor* must now be nearer to that of everyday life. But in the ages of faith they offered to God the most precious things they had. It was only in the village church that were to be seen just those things that do not belong to the everyday world: pieces of gold work, paintings, silks, lace, embroidery, and the statues of the Blessed Virgin crowned with jewels. Christians made financial sacrifices to honor Almighty God in the best way they could. All this was conducive to prayer and lifted up the soul. This is a natural proceeding for mankind: when the Three Magi went to visit the poor crib at Bethlehem they brought with them gold, frankincense and myrrh. Catholics are degraded by being made to pray in commonplace surroundings, multi-purpose halls that have nothing to distinguish them from any other public place, sometimes not even coming up to that. Here and there one finds a magnificent gothic or romanesque church abandoned and a sort of bare and dreary barn built to one side. Or else they organize "domestic eucharists" in dining rooms or even in kitchens. I have been told of one of these, celebrated in the home of a deceased person in the presence of his family and friends. After the ceremony the chalice was removed and then, on the same table covered with the same table cloth, they set up a buffet meal. At the same time, only a few hundred yards away, only the birds were singing to the Lord around the thirteenth-century church decorated with magnificent stained glass windows.

Those readers who remember the years before the war will certainly recall the fervor of the Corpus Christi processions with their numerous stations, the chants, the thuribles, the monstrance gleaming in the sun, carried by the priest under the gold-embroidered canopy; the banners, the flowers, the bells. The sense of adoration was born into the children's souls and ingrained there for life. This primordial aspect of prayer seems greatly neglected. Do I hear somebody still talking about necessary evolution and new habits of life? But traffic problems do not prevent street demonstrations, and the demonstrators are not inhibited about expressing their political opinions or their demands, whether just or not. Why should God alone be thrust aside, and why must only Christians refrain from rendering Him the public worship which is His due?

The almost total disappearance in France of processions is not caused by a lack of interest on the part of the faithful. It is proscribed by the new pastoral theory which, however, is ceaselessly urging the "active participation of the People of God." In 1969 a parish priest in the Oise section of France was expelled by his bishop who had forbidden the organizing of the traditional procession of Corpus Christi. The procession took place nevertheless and drew ten times more people than the village had inhabitants. Can one then say that the new pastoral style which is, in any case, in contradiction on this point with the conciliar Constitution on the Sacred Liturgy, is in accordance with the deep longings of those Christians who remain attached to such forms of piety?

And what are they offered in exchange? Very little, because services have been greatly reduced. Priests no longer offer the Holy Sacrifice each day; and when they do, they concelebrate, and the number of Masses has diminished accordingly. In country districts, it is practically impossible to attend Mass during the week; on Sundays a car is needed to travel out to the locality whose turn it is to receive the "sector priest." Many churches in France are permanently closed, others only opened a few times a year. Add to that the crisis in vocations, or rather the crisis in responding to vocations, and the practice of religion becomes yearly more difficult. The large towns are in general better served; but most of the time it is impossible to receive Communion, on First Fridays and First Saturdays of the month, for example. Naturally there is no longer any question of daily Mass; in many urban parishes Masses only take place by prior order, for a specific group at a pre-arranged time, and in such a manner that the passer-by coming in by chance feels himself to be a stranger at a celebration studded with allusions to the activities and life of the group. Discredit has been thrown upon what are called individual celebrations in opposition to community celebrations, but in reality the community has split into small cells. It is quite common for a priest to say Mass in the home of someone engaged in Catholic Action or other activities, in the presence of a group of activists. Or else one discovers the time-table for Sunday split up between different language groups; a Portuguese Mass, French Mass, Spanish Mass. In these times when foreign travel is commonplace Catholics find themselves attending Masses where they do not understand a single word, in spite of being told that it is not possible to pray without "participating." How could they?

No more Masses, or very few; no more processions, no more Benedictions of the Blessed Sacrament, no more Vespers. Public prayer is reduced to its most simple expression. Even when the faithful have overcome the difficulties of times and travelling, what will they find to slake their spiritual thirst? I will speak further on about the liturgy and the serious alterations it has undergone. For the moment, let us consider only the obvious outward appearances of public prayer. All too frequently, the atmosphere of the "celebration" offends Catholic religious feelings. There is the intrusion of secular rhythms with all kinds of percussion instruments, guitars and saxophones. A musician responsible for sacred music in a diocese of northern France, supported by a number of leading personalities in the world of music wrote:

> In spite of what it is currently called, the music of these songs is not modern: this musical style is not new, but has been played in the most profane places and surroundings (cabarets, music halls, often for more or less lascivious dances with foreign names). The people are led on to rock or swing. They all feel an urge to dance about. That sort of "body language" is certainly alien to our Western culture, unfavorable to contemplation and its origins are rather suspect. Most of the time our congregations, which already find it hard not to confuse the crochets and the quavers in a 6/8 bar, do not respect the rhythm; then one no longer feels like dancing, but with the rhythm gone to pieces, the habitual poorness of the melodic line becomes all the more noticeable.

What has happened to prayer in all of that? Happily it appears that in more than one place people have returned to less barbaric customs. People have then submitted, those who wish to sing, to the productions of official organizations specializing in Church music. For them, there is no question of making use of the marvellous heritage of past centuries. The usual melodies, always the same, are of a very different inspiration. The more elaborate pieces, executed by choirs, show a secular influence, and excite the feelings rather than penetrate the soul as plainchant does. The words are all new, using a new vocabulary, as if a flood twenty years ago had destroyed all the antiphonaries from which, even if they had wanted to make something new, they could have drawn inspiration; they adopt a style of the moment and are quickly outmoded, in a very short time being no longer comprehensible. Large numbers of recordings purposely designed for the animation of parishes give out paraphrases of the psalms and are frankly presented as such, thereby supplanting the sacred text of divine inspiration. Why not sing the psalms themselves?

A novelty appeared a little while ago: posters placed in church porches reading "to praise God, clap your hands." So during the celebration, at a sign from the leader, the congregation raised their hands above their heads and clapped rhythmically and loudly, producing an unfamiliar din within the sanctuary. This kind of innovation, unconnected even with our secular habits, which attempts to put an artificial action into the liturgy, will no doubt be gone tomorrow: it contributes however to discourage Catholics and to increase their confusion. Nobody is obliged to attend "Gospel Nights" but what can one do when the few Sunday Masses are infected with these lamentable practices?

The *pastorale d'ensemble* (ministry to the assembly) as they call it, constrains the faithful to adopt these new gestures in which they see no benefit and which go against their nature. Above all, everything must be done in a collective manner, with *èchanges* or sharing—of speech, of views, on the Gospel, and of handshakes, too. People go along with this half-heartedly, as statistics show. The very latest figures indicate a further falling off, from 1977 to 1983, in attendance at the Eucharist, whereas personal prayer shows a slight increase.[1] The *pastorale d'ensemble* has not, therefore won the people over. Here is what I read in a parish magazine in the Paris area:

> From time to time during the last two years the 9:30 a.m. Mass has been in a rather special style, inasmuch as

---

1. Poll *Madame Figaro—Sofres*, Sept. 1983. The first question was: "Do you go to communion once a week or more, or about once a month?"This corresponds more or less to attendance at Mass, since everybody now communicates. Replies in the affirmative had dropped from 16% to 9%.

the proclaiming of the Gospel was followed by an *èchange* for which those present formed groups of about ten persons. The first time this kind of celebration was tried, 69 people joined in sharing groups and 138 remained outside. One would have thought that with the help of time there would have been an improvement. This has not been the case. The parish team then organized a meeting to see whether or not to continue with the "Masses with Sharing."

One can understand how the two-thirds of the parishioners who had so far resisted the post-conciliar innovations were not enthusiastic about these improvised chatterings in the middle of Mass. How difficult it is to be a Catholic nowadays! The liturgy in French, even without "sharings," deafens the congregation with a flood of words so that many complain that they can no longer pray during Mass. When, then, will they pray?

The confused faithful are offered recipes which are always accepted by their bishops provided that they detach them from Christian spirituality. Yoga and Zen are the strangest, a disastrous orientalism which, claiming to lead to a "hygiene of the soul," directs devotion in false ways. Again, what about the abuses of "body language" which degrade the personality by exalting the body at the expense of elevation towards God? These new fashions, along with many others, have been introduced even into contemplative monasteries; and they are extremely dangerous. They show how right are those we hear say, "They are changing our religion."

III
What They Are Doing to the Mass

I have before me some photos published in Catholic newspapers representing the Mass as it is now often said. Looking at the first photo I find it difficult to understand at what moment of the Holy Sacrifice it has been taken. Behind an ordinary wooden table, which does not appear very clean and which has no cloth covering it, two persons wearing suits and ties elevate or present, one a chalice, the other a ciborium. The text informs me they are priests, one of them the federal chaplain of Catholic Action. On the same side of the table, close to the first celebrant are two girls wearing trousers, and near the second celebrant two boys in sweaters. A guitar is placed against a stool.

In another photo the scene is the corner of a room which might be the main room of a youth club. The priest is standing, wearing a Taizé-like alb, before a milking-stool which serves as an altar; there is a large earthenware bowl and a small mug of the same sort, together with two lighted candle-ends. Five young people are sitting cross-legged on the floor, one of them strumming a guitar.

The third photo shows an event which occurred a few years ago, the cruise of some ecologists who were seeking to prevent the French atomic experiments on the Isle of Mururoa. Amongst them was a priest who celebrated Mass on the deck of the sailing ship, in the company of two other men. All three were wearing shorts, one is even stripped to the waist. The priest is raising the Host, no doubt for the elevation. He is neither standing nor kneeling, but sitting or rather slumped against the boat's superstructure.

One common feature emerges from these scandalous pictures; the Eucharist is reduced to an everyday act, in commonplace surroundings, with commonplace utensils, attitudes and clothing. Now the so-called Catholic magazines which are sold on church bookstalls do not show these photos in order to criticize such ways, but on the contrary, to recommend them. *La Vie* even considers that that is not enough. Using in its habitual manner extracts from readers' letters to express its own thoughts without having them attributed to itself, it says, "The liturgical reform must go further . . . the unnecessary repetitions, the same form of words ever repeated, all this regulation holds back creativeness." What ought the Mass to be? The following gives a hint: "Our problems are manifold, our difficulties increasing and the Church still seems to be remote from them. Often we come out of Mass tired. There is a sort of gap between our daily life, our present worries, and the sort of life suggested to us on Sundays."

Certainly people come away tired from a Mass which strives to bring itself down to the level of mankind instead of raising them up to God, and which, because it is wrongly conceived does not permit them to rise above their "problems." The encouragement given to go even further demonstrates a deliberate intention to destroy what is sacred. The Catholic is there dispossessed of something which he needs and longs for, because he is drawn to honor and revere all which relate to God. How much more is this the case with the elements of the Sacrifice which are to become His Body and His Blood! Why make hosts that are grey or brown by leaving in part of the bran? Are they trying to make us forget that phrase omitted from the new Offertory: *hanc immaculatam hostiam*, this immaculate and spotless Host?

That, however, is merely a minor innovation. We frequently hear of the consecration of ordinary bread, leavened with yeast, instead of the pure wheat flour prescribed, the exclusive use of which has again been reiterated in the papal Instruction *Inaestimabile Donum*. All bounds have now been passed, there has even been an American bishop who recommends little cakes containing milk, eggs, baking-powder, honey and margarine. The desacralization extends to the persons vowed to the service of God, with the disappearance of the ecclesiastical habit for priests and religious, the use of Christian names, familiarity and a secularized way of living, all in the name of a new principle and not, as they have tried to make us believe, for practical needs. In proof of which I mention those nuns who leave their enclosure to live in rented flats in town, thereby doubling their expenses—abandoning the veil and incurring the cost of regular sessions at the hair dressers.

The loss of what is sacred leads also to sacrilege. A newspaper in the west of France informs us that the national contest for band-girls was held in 1980 in the Vendèe region of France. A Mass took place during which the band-girls danced and some of them then distributed Communion. Moreover, the ceremony was finished off with a rondelay in which the celebrant took part wearing priests' vestments. It is not my intention here to establish a catalogue of the abuses that are to be met with, but to give a few examples showing why Catholics today have so much at which to be perplexed and even scandalized. I am revealing nothing secret, the television has taken upon itself to spread in people's homes, during their Sunday morning programs, the inadmissible off-handedness that the bishops publicly display with regard to the Body of Christ: witness that Mass televised November 22, 1981, where the ciborium was replaced by baskets which the congregation passed from one to another to be finally placed on the floor with what remained of the Sacred Species!

In Poitiers on Holy Thursday the same year, a big spectacular celebration consisted of the indiscriminate consecration of loaves and jugs of wine upon the tables from which everyone came and helped himself.

Concerts of secular music held in churches are now generalized. Places of worship are even made available for rock music events, with all the excesses that these habitually involve. Some churches and cathedrals have been given over to debauchery, drugs and filth of all kinds, and it is not the local clergy who have then performed ceremonies of expiation but groups of the faithful rightly digusted by these scandals. How can the bishops and priests who have encouraged these things not fear to bring down divine punishment upon themselves and their people? It is already apparent in the fruitlessness of their work. It is all wasted because the Holy Sacrifice of the Mass, desecrated as it is, no longer confers grace and no longer transmits it. The contempt for the Real Presence of Christ in the Eucharist is the most flagrant sign by which the new mentality, no longer Catholic, expresses itself. Even without going as far as the rowdy excesses I have just mentioned, this is noticeable every day. The Council of Trent explained without any possible doubt that Our Lord is present in the smallest particles of the consecrated bread. What are we to think then of Communion in the hand? When a Communion plate is used, even if the Communions are few in number, there are always particles remaining. In consequence, the particles now remain in the communicant's hands. The faith of many is shaken by this, especially that of children.

The new way can only have one explanation: if people come to Mass to break the bread of friendship, of the community meal, of the common faith, then it is quite natural that no excessive precautions should be taken. If the Eucharist is a symbol expressing simply the memory of a past event and the spiritual presence of Our Lord, it is quite logical not to worry about a few crumbs which may fall on the floor. But if it is a matter of the presence of God Himself, our Creator, as the faith of the Church would have it, how can we understand that such practices be allowed and even encouraged, in spite of documents fresh from Rome? The idea which they are endeavoring to insinuate in this way is a Protestant one against which Catholics not yet contaminated are rebelling. To impose it more effectively, the faithful are obliged to communicate standing.

Is it fitting that when we go to receive Christ before whom, says St. Paul, every knee shall bow, in heaven, on

earth and under the earth, we should do so without the
least sign of respect or allegiance? Many priests no longer
genuflect before the Holy Eucharist; the new rite of Mass
encourages this. I can see only two possible reasons: either
an immense pride which makes us treat God as if we were
His equals, or else the certitude that He is not really present
in the Eucharist.

Am I just getting up a case against the so-called Conciliar Church? No, I am not inventing anything. Listen to
the way the Dean of the Faculty of Theology of Strasbourg
expresses himself:

> We also speak of the presence of a speaker or of an
> actor, meaning thereby a quality different from a simply
> geographical "being there." After all, someone can be pre-
> sent by a symbolic act which he does not accomplish physi-
> cally but which other people accomplish by creative fidelity
> to his fundamental intention. For example, the Festival of
> Bayreuth realizes without doubt a presence of Richard
> Wagner which is greatly superior in intensity to that which
> may be manifested by occasional recitals or concerts de-
> voted to his music. It is within this last perspective, it
> seems to me, that we should place the eucharistic presence
> of Christ.

To compare the Mass with the Bayreuth Festival! No,
we certainly do not agree—either regarding the words or
the music!

IV

The Mass of All Time Versus
The Mass of Our Time

In preparation for the 1981 Eucharistic Congress, a questionnaire was distributed, the first question of which was: "Of these two definitions: 'The Holy Sacrifice of the Mass' and 'Eucharistic Meal,' which one do you adopt spontaneously?" There is a great deal that could be said about this way of questioning Catholics, giving them to some extent the choice and appealing to their private judgment on a subject where spontaneity has no place. The definition of the Mass is not chosen in the same way that one chooses a political party.

Alas! The insinuation does not result from a blunder on the part of the person who drew up the questionnaire. One has to accept that the liturgical reform tends to replace the idea and the reality of the Sacrifice by the reality of a meal. That is how one comes to speak of eucharistic celebration, or of a "Supper"; but the expression "Sacrifice" is much less used. It has almost totally disappeared from catechism handbooks just as it has from sermons. It is absent from Canon II, attributed to St. Hippolytus.

This tendency is connected with what we have discovered concerning the Real Presence: if there is no longer a sacrifice, there is no longer any need for a victim. The victim is present in view of the sacrifice. To make of the Mass a memorial or fraternal meal is the Protestant error. What happened in the sixteenth century? Precisely what is taking place today. Right from the start they replaced the altar by a table, removed the crucifix from it, and made the "president of the assembly" turn around to face the congregation. The setting of the Protestant Lord's Supper is found in *Pierres Vivantes*, the prayer book prepared by the bishops in France which all children attendingcatechism are obliged to use:

> "Christians meet together to celebrate the Eucharist. It is the Mass . . . They proclaim the faith of the Church, they pray for the whole world, they offer the bread and the wine. The priest who presides at the assembly says the great prayer of thanksgiving."

Now in the Catholic religion it is the priest who celebrates Mass; it is he who offers the bread and wine. The notion of president has been borrowed directly from Protestantism. The vocabulary follows the change of ideas. Formerly, we would say, "Monsignor Lustiger will celebrate a Pontifical Mass." I am told that at Radio Notre Dame, the phrase used at present is, "Jean-Marie Lustiger will preside at a concelebration." Here is how they speak about Mass in a brochure issued by the Conference of Swiss Bishops: "The Lord's Supper achieves firstly communion with Christ. It is the same communion that Jesus brought about during His life on earth when He sat at table with sinners, and has been continued in the Eucharistic meal since the day of the Resurrection. The Lord invites His friends to come together and He will be present among them."

To that every Catholic is obliged to reply in a categoric manner, "NO! the Mass is not that!" It is not the continuation of a meal similar to that which Our Lord invited Saint Peter and a few of his disciples one morning on the lakeside, after His Resurrection. "When they came to land they saw a charcoal fire there and a fish laid thereon and bread. Jesus said them, come and dine. And none of them durst ask Him, 'Who art thou?', knowing that it was the Lord. And Jesus cometh and taketh the bread and giveth them, and fish in like manner" (John 21: 9-13).

The communion of the priest and the faithful is a communion in the Victim Who has offered Himself up on the altar of sacrifice. This is of solid stone; if not it contains at least the altar stone which is a stone of sacrifice. Within are laid relics of the martyrs because they have offered their blood for their Master. This communion of the Blood of Our Lord with the blood of the martyrs encourages us also to offer up our lives.

If the Mass is a meal, I understand the priest turning towards the congregation. One does not preside at a meal with one's back to the guests. But a sacrifice is offered to God, not to the congregation. This is the reason why the priest as the head of the faithful turns toward God and the crucifix over the altar.

At every opportunity emphasis is laid on what the New Sunday Missal calls the "Narrative of the Institution." The Jean-Bart Center, the official center for the Archdiocese of Paris, states, "At the center of the Mass, there is a narrative." Again, no! The Mass is not a narrative, it is an *action*.

Three indispensable conditions are needed for it to be the continuation of the Sacrifice of the Cross: the oblation of the victim, the transubstantiation which renders the victim present effectively and not symbolically, and the celebration by a priest, consecrated by his priesthood, in place of the High Priest Who is Our Lord.

Likewise the Mass can obtain the remission of sins. A simple memorial, a narrative of the institution accompanied by a meal, would be far from sufficient for this. All the supernatural virtue of the Mass comes from its relationship to the Sacrifice of the Cross. If we no longer believe that, then we no longer believe anything about Holy Church, the Church would not longer have any reason for existing, we would no longer claim to be Catholics. Luther understood very clearly that the Mass is the heart and soul of the Church. He said: "Let us destroy the Mass and we shall destroy the Church."

Now we can see that the *Novus Ordo Missae*, that is to say, the New Order adopted after the Council, has been drawn up on Protestant lines, or at any rate dangerously close to them. For Luther, the Mass was a sacrifice of praise, that is to say, an act of praise, an act of thanksgiving, but certainly not an expiatory sacrifice which renews and applies the Sacrifice of the Cross. For him, the Sacrifice of the Cross took place at a given moment of history, it is the prisoner of that history; we can only apply to ourselves Christ's merits by our faith in His death and resurrection. Contrarily, the Church maintains that this Sacrifice is realized mystically upon our altars at each Mass, in an unbloody manner by the separation of the Body and the Blood under the species of bread and wine. This renewal allows the merits of the Cross to be applied to the faithful there present, perpetuating this source of grace in time and in space. The Gospel of St. Matthew ends with these words: "And behold, I am with you all days, even until the end of the world."

The difference in conception is not slender. Efforts are being made to reduce it, however, by the alteration of Catholic doctrine of which we can see numerous signs in the liturgy.

Luther said, "Worship used to be addressed to God as a homage. Henceforth it will be addressed to man to console and enlighten him. The sacrifice used to have pride of place but the sermon will supplant it." That signified the introduction of the Cult of Man, and in the Church, the importance accorded to the "Liturgy of the Word." If we open the new missals, this revolution has been accomplished in them too. A reading has been added to the two which existed, together with a "universal prayer" often utilized for propagating political or social ideas; taking the homily into account, we often end up with a shift of balance towards the "word." Once the sermon is ended, the Mass is very close to its end.

Within the Church, the priest is marked with an indelible character which makes of him and *alter Christus:* he alone can offer the Holy Sacrifice. Luther considered the distinction between clergy and laity to the "first wall raised up by the Romanists"; all Christians are priests, the pastor is only exercising a function in presiding at the Evangelical Mass. In the *Novus Ordo*, the "I" of the celebrant has been replaced by "we"; it is written everywhere that the faithful "celebrate," they are associated with the acts of worship, they read the epistle and occasionally the Gospel, give out Communion, sometimes preach the homily, which may be replaced by "a dialogue by small groups upon the Word of God," meeting together beforehand to "construct" the Sunday celebration. But this is only a first step; for several years we have heard of those responsible for diocesan organizations who have been putting forward propositions of this nature: "It is not the ministers but the assembly who celebrate" (handouts by the National Center for Pastoral Liturgy), or "The assembly is the prime subject of the liturgy"; what matters is not the "functioning of the rites but the image the assembly gives to itself and the relationship the co-celebrants create between themselves" (P. Gelineau, architect of the liturgical reform and professor at the Paris Catholic Institute). If it is the assembly which matters then it is understandable that private Masses should be discredited, which means that priests no longer say them because it is less and less easy to find an assembly, above all during the week. It is a breach with the unchanging doctrine: that the Church needs a multiplicity of Sacrifices of the Mass, both for the application of the Sacrifice of the Cross and for all the objects assigned to it, adoration, thanksgiving, propitiation,[2] and impetration.[3]

As if that were not enough, the objective of some is to eliminate the priest entirely, which has given rise to the notorious ADAP (Sunday Assemblies in the Absence of the Priest). We can imagine the faithful gathering to pray together in order to honor the Lord's Day; but these ADAP are in reality a sort of "dry Mass," lacking only the consecration; and the lack, as one can read in a document of the Regional Center for Social and Religious Studies at Lille, is only because *"until further instructions* lay people do not

---

2. The action of rendering God propitious.
3. The action of obtaining divine graces and blessings.

have the power to carry out this act." The absence of the
priest may even be intentional "so that the faithful can learn
to manage for themselves." Father Gelineau in *Demain la
Liturgie* writes that the ADAP are only an "educational tran-
sition until such time as mentalities have changed," and he
concludes with disconcerting logic that there are still too
many priests in the Church, "too many doubtless for things
to evolve quickly."

Luther suppressed the Offertory; why offer the pure
and Immaculate Host if there is no more sacrifice? In the
French *Novus Ordo* the Offertory is practically non-existent;
besides which it no longer has this name. The New Sunday
Missal speaks of the "prayers of presentation." The formula
used reminds one more of a thanksgiving, a thank-you, for
the fruits of the earth. To realize this fully, it is sufficient to
compare it with the formulas traditionally used by the
Church in which clearly appears the propitiatory and expiatory nature of the Sacrifice "which I offer Thee for my innumerable sins, offenses and negligences, for all those here
present and for all Christians living and dead, that it may
avail for my salvation and theirs for eternal life." Raising
the chalice, the priest then says, "We offer Thee, Lord, the
chalice of Thy redemption, imploring Thy goodness to accept it like a sweet perfume into the presence of Thy divine
Majesty for our salvation and that of the whole world."

What remains of that in the New Mass? This: "Blessed
are You, Lord, God of the universe, You who give us this
bread, fruit of the earth and work of human hands. We offer it to You; it will become the bread of life," and the same
for the wine which will become "our spiritual drink." What
purpose is served by adding, a little further on: "Wash me
of my faults, Lord. Purify me of my sin," and "may our
sacrifice today find grace before You"? Which sin? Which
sacrifice? What connection can the faithful make between
this vague presentation of the offerings and the redemption
that he is looking forward to? I will ask another question:
Why substitute for a text that is clear and whose meaning is
complete, a series of enigmatic and loosely bound phrases?

If a need is found for change, it should be for something better. These incidental phrases which seem to make up for the insufficiency of the "prayers of presentation" remind us of Luther, who was at pains to arrange the changes with caution. He retained as much as possible of the old ceremonies, limiting himself to changing their meaning. The Mass, to a great extent, kept its external appearance, the people found in the churches nearly the same setting, nearly the same rites, with slight changes made to please them, because from then on people were consulted much more than before; they were much more aware of their importance in matters of worship, taking a more active part by means of chant and praying aloud. Little by little Latin gave way to German.

Doesn't all this remind you of something? Luther was also anxious to ceate new hymns to replace "all the mumblings of popery." Reforms always adopt the appearance of a cultural revolution.

In the *Novus Ordo* the most ancient parts of the Roman Canon which goes back to apostolic times has been reshaped to bring it closer to the Lutheran formula of consecration, with both an addition and a suppression. The translation in French has gone even further by altering the meaning of the words *pro multis*. Instead of "My blood which shall be shed for you and for many," we read "which shall be shed for you and for the multitude." This does not mean the same thing and theologically is not without significance.

You may have noticed that most priests nowadays recite as one continuous passage the principal part of the Canon which begins, "the night before the Passion He took bread in His holy hands," without observing the pause implied by the rubric of the Roman Missal: "Holding with both hands the host between the index finger and the thumb, he pronounces the words of the Consecration in a low but distinct voice and attentively over the host." The tone changes, becomes intimatory, the five words *"Hoc est enim Corpus Meum,"* operate the miracle of transubstantiation, as do those that are said for the consecration of the wine. The

new Missal asks the celebrant to keep to the narrative tone
of voice as if he were indeed proceeding with a memorial.
Creativity being now the rule, we see some celebrants who
recite the text while showing the Host all around or even
breaking it in an ostentatious manner so as to add the gesture to their words and better illustrate their text. The two
genuflections out of the four having been suppressed, those
which remain being sometimes omitted, we have to ask
ourselves if the priest in fact has the feeling of consecrating,
even supposing that he really does have the intention to do
so.

Then, from being puzzled Catholics you become worried Catholics: is the Mass at which you have assisted
valid? Is the Host you have received truly the Body of
Christ?

It is a grave problem. How can the ordinary faithful decide? For the validity of a Mass there exists essential conditions: matter, form, intention and the validly ordained
priest. If these conditions are filled one cannot see how to
conclude invalidity. The prayers of the Offertory, the Canon
and the Priest's Communion are necessary for the integrity
of the Sacrifice and the Sacrament, but not for its validity.
Cardinal Mindzenty pronouncing in secret in his prison the
words of Consecration over a little bread and wine, so as to
nourish himself with the Body and Blood of Our Lord without being seen by his guards, was certainly accomplishing
the Sacrifice and the Sacrament.

A Mass celebrated with the American bishop's honey-
cakes of which I have spoken is certainly invalid, like those
where the words of the Consecration are seriously altered
or even omitted. I am not inventing anything, a case has
been recorded where a celebrant went to such an extent of
creativity that he quite simply forgot the Consecration! But
how can we assess the intention of the priest? It is obvious
that there are fewer and fewer valid Masses as the faith of
priests becomes corrupted and they no longer have the intention to do what the Church—which cannot change her
intention—has always done. The present-day training of

those who are called seminarians does not prepare them to accomplish valid Masses. They are no longer taught to consider the Holy Sacrifice as the essential action of their priestly life.

Furthermore it can be said without any exaggeration whatsoever, that the majority of Masses celebrated without altar stones, with common vessels, leavened bread, with the introduction of profane words into the very body of the Canon, etc., are sacrilegious, and they prevent faith by diminishing it. The desacralization is such that these Masses can come to lose their supernatural character, "the mystery of faith," and become no more than acts of natural religion.

Your perplexity takes perhaps the following form: may I assist at a sacrilegious Mass which is nevertheless valid, in the absence of any other, in order to satisfy my Sunday obligation? The answer is simple: these Masses cannot be the object of an obligation; we must moreover apply to them the rules of moral theology and canon law as regards the participation or the attendance at an action which endangers the faith or may be sacrilegious.

The New Mass, even when said with piety and respect for the liturgical rules, is subject to the same reservations since it is impregnated with the spirit of Protestantism. It bears within it a poison harmful to the faith. That being the case, the French Catholic of today finds himself in the conditions of religious practice which prevail in missionary countries. There, the inhabitants in some regions are able to attend Mass only three or four times a year. The faithful of our country should make the effort to attend once each month at the Mass of All Time, the true source of grace and sanctification, in one of those places where it continues to be held in honor.

I owe it to truth to say and affirm without fear of error that the Mass codified by St. Pius V—and not invented by him, as some often say—express clearly these three realities: sacrifice, Real Presence, and the priesthood of the clergy. It takes into account also, as the Council of Trent has pointed out, the nature of mankind which needs outside help to raise itself to meditation upon divine things. The established customs have not been made at random, they cannot be overthrown or abruptly abolished with impunity. How many of the faithful, how many young priests, how many bishops, have lost the faith since the introduction of these reforms! One cannot thwart nature and faith without their taking their revenge.

But as it happens, we are told, man is no longer what he was a century ago; his nature has been changed by the technical civilization in which he is immersed. How absurd! The innovators take good care not to reveal to the faithful their desire to fall into line with Protestantism. They invoke another argument: change. Here is how they explain it at the theological evening school in Strasbourg: "We must recognize that today we are confronted with a veritable cultural mutation. One particular manner of celebrating the memorial of the Lord was bound up with a religious universe which is no longer ours." It is quickly said, and everything disappears. We must start again from scratch. Such are the sophisms they use to make us change our faith. What is a "religious universe"? It would be better to be frank and say: "a religion which is no longer ours."

V
"You're a Dinosaur!"

Catholics who feel that radical transformations are taking place have difficulty in standing up against the relentless propaganda they encounter (and which is common to all revolutions). They are told, "You can't accept change. Yet change is a part of life. You're static. What was good fifty years ago isn't suitable to today's mentality or way of life. You're hung up on the past. You can't change your ways!" Many have given in to the reform to avoid this criticism, unable to find an argument against the sneering charge, "You're a reactionary, a dinosaur. You can't move with the times!"

Cardinal Ottaviani said of the bishops, "They are afraid of looking old."

But we have never refused certain changes, adaptations that bear witness to the vitality of the Church. In the liturgy, people my age have seen some of these. Shortly after I was born, St. Pius X made some improvements, especially in giving more importance to the temporal cycle in the missal, in lowering the age for First Communion for children and in restoring liturgical chant, which had fallen into disuse. Pius XII came along and reduced the length of the eucharistic fast because of difficulties inherent in modern life. For the same reason he authorized afternoon and evening Masses, put the Office of the Paschal Vigil on the evening of Holy Saturday and rearranged the services of Holy Week in general. John XXIII, before the Council, added his own touches to the so-called rite of St. Pius V.

But none of this came anywhere near to what happened

in 1969, when a new concept of the Mass was introduced.

We are also criticized for being attached to external forms of secondary importance, like Latin. This is a dead language, they tell us, which no one understands—as if Christians understood it in the sixteenth or nineteenth centuries. Such negligence on the part of the Church (in this view) in waiting so long to get rid of Latin! I think the Church had her reasons. Yet we should not be surprised that Catholics feel the need of a greater understanding of the sacred texts, from which they draw spiritual nourishment, and that they want to be more intimately involved in the action taking place in front of them.

It was not to satisfy these desires, however, that the vernacular was introduced from one end of the Holy Sacrifice to the other. Reading the Epistle and Gospel in the vernacular is an improvement and is practised at St. Nicholas du Chardonnet in Paris and in the priories of the Society which I founded. To go any further would mean losing far more than would be gained, because understanding the texts is not the ultimate purpose of prayer, nor even the only means of putting the soul in a state of prayer, i.e., in union with God. If too much attention is given to the meaning of the words, they can even be an obstacle.

I am surprised that this is not understood, especially when we hear so much talk these days about a religion of the heart, less intellectual and more spontaneous. Union with God can be achieved as much by beautiful, heavenly music as by the general ambience of liturgical action: the sanctity and religious feel of the place, or its architectural beauty, or the fervor of the Christian community, or the dignity and devotion of the celebrant, or symbolic decorations, or the fragrance of the incense. Moving about is unimportant, as long as the soul is uplifted. All you need to prove this is to go into a Benedictine monastery which has kept the divine worship in all its splendor.

But this does not lessen in the least the need to seek a better understanding of the prayers and hymns as well as a more perfect participation. But it is a mistake to try to reach the goal purely and simply by bringing in the vernacular and totally suppressing the universal language of the Church, as has unfortunately happened almost everywhere in the world. We need only look at the success of Masses, even in the *Novus Ordo* rite, which have kept the chant for the *Credo*, the *Sanctus*, or the *Agnus Dei*.

Latin is a universal language. In using it, the liturgy forms us into a universal, i.e., Catholic, communion. By contrast, localizing and individualizing the liturgy robs it of this dimension which can make such a deep impression on souls. To avoid making such a mistake, it should be enough to observe the Eastern rites, in which the liturgical action has long been couched in the vernacular. And there an isolation can be seen—from which members of these communities suffer. When they scatter far and wide from their homelands, they need their own priests for the Mass, the sacraments and ceremonies of all kinds. They build special churches, which, in the nature of things, separate them from the rest of the Catholic population.

What do they gain from this? It is not entirely clear that having their own liturgical language has made them more fervent in practising their faith than people benefitting from a universal language, not understood by man, perhaps, but easy enough to translate.

If we look outside the Church, we may ask how Islam has succeeded in keeping its cohesiveness while spreading over regions as different and among peoples of such diverse races as in Turkey, North Africa, Indonesia and black Africa. It has succeeded in imposing Arabic everywhere as the single language of the Koran. In Africa, I saw marabouts teachings children to recite the sacred texts by heart when they could not understand a single word of them. Islam goes so far as to forbid the translation of this holy book. It is fashionable these days to admire the religion of Mohammed: thousands of French people, it is said, are converting to it and taking up collections in the churches to build mosques in France. We would do well, however, simply to take note of one example which we should remember: the sustaining power of a single language for prayer and worship.

The fact that Latin is a dead language is in its favor: it is the best means of protecting the expression of faith against linguistic changes which take place naturally in the course of time. The study of semantics has developed rapidly in the last ten years or so: it has even been introduced into French language courses in the schools. Semantics investigates changes in the meaning of words, the gradual shift of signification in the passage of time and often over very short periods. Let us make use of this branch of knowledge, therefore, to understand the danger of handing over the deposit of faith to changing ways of speaking. Do you believe that we could have kept intangible, eternal truths free of corruption for two thousand years if they were expressed in languages that are constantly evolving and which differ from one country and even from one region to another? Living languages change and fluctuate. If we put the liturgy into any one of them at any time, we will have to be continually adapting according to semantic requirements. So it is not surprising that there must be endless committees set up for this, and that priests no longer have time to say Mass.

When I went to see His Holiness Pope Paul VI at Castelgandolfo in 1976, I said to him, "I do not know if you are aware, Your Holiness, that there are now officially thirteen Eucharistic prayers in France." The Pope raised his arms heavenward and exclaimed, "More than that, Excellency, more than that!" This gives me the basis for asking, would there be so many if the liturgists were required to compose in Latin? Besides these formulas put into circulation—after being printed here, there or anywhere—we would have to mention also the canons improvised by the priest during the celebration and everything he introduces from the "penitential preparation" to the "dismissal of the assembly." Do you think he could do this if he had to officiate in Latin?

Another external sign against which opinion has solidified is the wearing of the cassock—not so much in church or in visits to the Vatican as in everyday life. The question is not of the most fundamental importance, yet it has great symbolic value. Every time the Pope mentions this—and Pope John Paul II has done so repeatedly—howls of protest are heard from the ranks of the clergy. In this connection I read in a Paris newspaper this statement from an *avant-garde* priest: "This is childishness . . . in France, wearing a recognizable uniform is meaningless, because there is no need to recognize a priest on the street. Quite the contrary: the cassock or Roman collar creates a barrier . . . the priest is a man like anyone else. Of course he is president of the Eucharistic Assembly!"

This "president of the Eucharistic assembly" is here expressing ideas that are contrary to the Gospel and to clearly recognized social realities. In all religions, leaders wear distinctive signs. Anthropology, which is now all the rage, is there to prove it. Among Muslims you see differences in dress: collars and rings. Buddhist monks wear saffron-colored robes and shave their heads. Young people associated with this religion can be seen on the streets of Paris and other large cities, and their appearance evokes no criticism.

The habit identifies the cleric or the religious, as a uniform identifies a soldier or a policeman. But with a difference: these latter, in representing the civil order, remain citizens like other people, whereas the priest is supposed to keep his distinctive habit in all phases of life. In fact, the sacred mark he received at ordination means that he is in the world but not of the world. We know this from St. John: "You are not of the world; I chose you out of the world" (15.19). His habit should be distinctive and at the same time reflect the spirit of modesty, discretion and poverty.

Secondly, the priest has the duty to bear witness to Our Lord. "You are My witness . . . men do not put a lamp under a bushel." Religion should not be confined to the sacristy—as the powers in Eastern European countries have long since declared it should be. Christ commanded us to spread our faith, to make it visible by a witness which should be seen and understood by all. The witness of the word, which is certainly more essential to the priest than the witness of the cassock, is nevertheless greatly facilitated by the unmistakable sign of the priesthood implicit in the wearing of the soutane.

Separation of Church and State, which is accepted and sometimes considered preferable, has helped the spirit of atheism to penetrate little by little into all the realms of activity, and we must admit that many Catholics and even priests no longer have a very clear idea of the place of the Catholic religion in civil society. Secularism is everywhere.

The priest who lives in a society of this type gets the ever increasing impression of being a stranger in this society, an embarrassment, and finally a symbol of a past age, doomed to disappear. His presence is barely tolerated. At least that is the way he sees it. Hence his wish to identify with the secular world, to lose himself in the crowd. What is lacking in priests of this type is experience of less dechristianized countries than theirs. What is especially lacking in them is a profound sense of their priesthood.

It is therefore difficult to make judgments on the religious spirit of the day. It is unfair to assume that those whom we meet in business relations or in informal relations are not religious. The young priests who come out of Ecône and all who have not gone along with the fad of anonymity verify this every day. Barrier? Quite the contrary. People stop them on the street, in stations, to talk to them, often quite simply to say what a joy it is for them to see a priest. The great boast of the new Church is dialogue. But how can this begin if we hide from the eyes of our prospective dialogue partners? In Communist countries the first act of the dictators is to forbid the cassock; this is part of a program to stamp out religion. And we must believe the reverse to be true too. The priest who declares his identity by his exterior appearance is a living sermon. The absence of recognizable priests in a large city is a serious step backward in the preaching of the Gospel. It is a continuation of the wicked work of the Revolution and the Laws of Separation.

It should be added that the soutane keeps the priest out

of trouble for it imposes an attitude on him, it reminds him at every minute of his mission on earth. It protects him from temptations. A priest in a cassock has no identity crisis. As for the faithful, they know what they are dealing with; the cassock is a guarantee of the authenticity of the priesthood. Catholics have told me of the difficulty they feel in going to confession to a priest in a business suit; it gives them the impression they are confiding the secrets of their conscience to some sort of nobody. Confession is a judicial act; hence the civil law feels the need to put robes on its magistrates.

VI
The New Forms of Baptism, Marriage, Penance and Extreme Unction

The Catholic, whether he be regularly practising or one who goes to church for the great moments of life, finds himself asking such basic questions as, "What is baptism?"

It is a new phenomenon, for not so long ago anyone could answer that, and anyway, nobody asked the question. The first effect of baptism is the redemption from original sin; that was known from father to son and mother to daughter.

But now nobody any longer talks about it anywhere. The simplified ceremony which takes place in the church speaks of sin in a context which seems to refer to that which the person being baptized will commit during his or her life, and not the original fault that we are all born with.

Baptism from then on simply appears as a sacrament which unites us to God, or rather makes us members of the community. This is the explanation of the "rite of welcome" that is imposed in some places as an initial step, in a first ceremony. It is not due to any private initiative since we discover plenty of variations upon baptism by stages in the leaflets of the National Center of Pastoral Liturgy. It is called "deferred baptism." After the welcome comes the "progression," the "seeking." The sacrament will be administered, or not administered, when the child is able, according to the terms used, to choose freely, which may occur at quite an advanced age, eighteen years or more. A professor of dogmatic theology, highly esteemed in the new Church, has established a distinction between those Christians whose faith and religious culture he is confident he can verify, and the others—more than three-quarters of the total— to whom he attributes only a supposed faith when they request baptism for their children. These Christians "of the popular religion" are detected during the preparatory meetings and dissuaded from proceeding any farther than the "ceremony of welcome." This method of going on is "more appropriate to the cultural situation of our civilization."

Recently a parish priest in the Somme department who had to enroll two children for their First Communion asked for their baptismal certificates, which were sent to him from the family's parish of origin. He then found that one of the children had been baptized but not the other, contrary to what the parents believed. This is the sort of situation that results from such practices. What they give is in effect only a semblance of baptism which those present take in good faith to be the true sacrament.

That you should find this disconcerting is quite understandable. You have also to face up to a specious argument which even appears in parish magazines, generally in the way of suggestions or testimonies signed with Christian names, that is to say anonymously. We read in one of them that Alan and Evelyn state, "Baptism is not a magic rite which will efface by miracle any original sin. We believe that salvation is total, free, and for all: God has elected all men in His love, on any condition, or rather without condition. For us, to be baptized is to decide to change our life, it is a personal commitment that no one can make for you. It is a conscious decision which implies preliminary instruction, etc." What frightful errors are contained in those few lines! They lead to the justifying of another method; the suppression of infant baptism. It is another alignment with the Protestants, in defiance of the teachings of the Church right from its beginnings, as St. Augustine wrote in the fourth century: "The custom of baptizing children is not a recent innovation but the faithful repetition of apostolic tradition. This custom by itself alone and without any written document, constitutes the certain rule of truth." The Council of Carthage, in the year 251, prescribed that baptism should be conferred on infants "even before they are eight days old," and the Congregation for the Doctrine of the Faith issued a reminder of the obligation in its Instruction *Pastoralis actio*, on November 21, 1980, basing it upon "a norm of immemorial tradition."

That is a thing you should know so as to be able to insist upon a sacred right when someone attempts to refuse your newborn children their share in the life of grace. Parents do not wait until their child is eighteen years old before deciding for him his diet, or to have a necessary surgical operation. Within the supernatural order their duty is even greater, and the faith which presides at the sacrament when the child is not capable of taking on for himself a personal engagement is the responsibility you would have in depriving your child of eternal life in Paradise. Our Lord Himself has said in a most clear manner, "No one, unless he be born again of water and the Holy Ghost can enter into the Kingdom of God."

The results of this peculiar pastoral practice were quick to appear. In the diocese of Paris, whereas one child out of two was baptized in 1965, only one child in four was baptized in 1976. The clergy of one suburban parish observed, without appearing concerned about it, that there were 450 baptisms in 1965 and 150 in 1976. From the whole of France, the fall continues. From 1970 to 1981, the overall figure dropped from 596,673 to 530,385, while the population increased by more than three million during the same period.

All this is the outcome of having falsified the definition of baptism. As soon as they stopped saying that baptism wipes out original sin, people have been asking, "What is baptism?" and straightaway after, "What is the good of baptism?" If they have not got as far as that, they have at least thought about the arguments that have been put to them and accepted that there was no urgency, and after all, at the age of adolescence the child could decide for himself and join the Christian community in the same way as joining a political party or a union.

The question is raised in the same way regarding marriage. Marriage has always been defined by its first aim which is procreation and its secondary aim which is married love. Now, at the Council they sought to alter this definition and say there was no longer a primary aim, but that the two aims of which I speak were equivalent. It was Cardinal Suenens who proposed this change and I still remember Cardinal Brown, the Master General of the Dominicans, getting up to say, "*Caveatis! Caveatis!*—Beware! Beware! If we accept this definition we go against all the tradition of the Church and we pervert the meaning of marriage. We do not have the right to modify the Church's traditional definitions."

He quoted texs in support of his warning and there was great agitation in the nave of St. Peter's. Cardinal Suenens was pressed by the Holy Father to moderate the terms he had used and even to change them. The Pastoral Constitution, *Gaudium et Spes*, contains nevertheless an ambiguous passage, where emphasis is laid on procreation "without nevertheless minimizing the other aims of marriage." The Latin verb, *post habere*, permits the translation "without putting in second place the other aims of marriage," which would mean "to place them all on the same level." This is what is wanted nowadays; all that is said about marriage comes back to the false idea expressed by Cardinal Suenens, that conjugal love—which was soon termed quite simply and much more crudely "sexuality"—comes at the head of the purposes of marriage. Consequently, under the heading of sexuality, everything is permitted—contraception, family planning and finally abortion.

One bad definition, and we are plunged into total disorder. The Church, in her traditional liturgy, has the priest say, "Lord, in Thy goodness, assist the institutions Thou hast established for the propagation of the human race . . ." She has chosen the passage from the Epistle of St. Paul to the Ephesians, which points out the duties of the married couple, making of their joint relationship an image of the relationship uniting Christ and His Church. Very often the couple to be married are nowadays invited to make up their own Mass without even having to choose the Epistle from Holy Scripture, replacing it by a profane text, and taking a reading from the Gospel that has no connection with the sacrament to be received. The priest in his exhortation takes good care not to mention the demands to which they will have to submit, for fear of giving a forbidding impression of the Church or even of offending any divorced people present among the congregation.

Just as for baptism, experiments have been made for marriages by stages, or non-sacramental marriage, which scandalize Catholics. These experiments, tolerated by the episcopate, take place following lines laid down by the official organizations and are encouraged by diocesan officials. A form put out by the Jean Bart Center shows some of the ways of going about it. Here is one:

> A reading from the text: "The essential is invisible to the eyes" (Epistle of St. Peter). There is no exchange of vows but a liturgy of the hands, symbol of labor and workers' solidarity. Exchange of rings (without the blessing), in silence. Reference to Robert's work: welding, soldering (he is a plumber). The kiss. The Our Father by all the believers in the congregation. Hail Mary. The newlyweds lay a bouquet of flowers at the statue of Mary.

Why would Our Lord have instituted the sacraments if they were to be replaced by this kind of ceremony devoid of everything supernatural, excepting the two prayers at the end? A few years ago we heard a lot about liturgy in the department of Saone-et-Loire. To justify this "Liturgy of Welcome," it was said that they wished to give young couples the desire to come back later and get married for good. Out of something like two hundred pseudo-marriages, two years later not a single couple had returned to regularize their position. Even if they had, the fact would remain that the priest of this parish had actually recognized officially, if not actually blessed, over a period of two years, something none other than concubinage. An official Church survey has revealed that in Paris 23% of the parishes had already held non-sacramental weddings for couples, one of whom if not both were non-believers, for the purpose of gratifying the families, or the couples themselves, often out of concern for social conformity.

It goes without saying that a Catholic does not have the right to attend such goings-on. As for the so-called married couple, they can always say they have been to church and doubtless they will end up by believing their situation to be regular by dint of seeing their friends follow the same path. Misguided Catholics will wonder if it is not better than nothing. Indifference takes over; they become willing to accept any arrangement, from a simple registry-office wedding to juvenile cohabitation (in respect of which so many parents want to show themselves to be "understanding"), and finally through to free unions. Total de-christianization lies ahead; the couples each lack the graces which come from the sacrament of marriage in order to bring up their children, if at least they agree to have any. The breakdowns in these unsanctified households have increased to such an extent as to worry the Council of Economic and Social Affairs, of which a recent report shows that even a secular society is aware that it is heading for ruin as a result of the instability of these families or pseudo-families.

Then there is the sacrament of Extreme Unction. This is no longer the sacrament of the sick or the feeble. It has become the sacrament of the old: some priests administer it to persons of pensionable age who show no particular sign of approaching death. It is no longer the sacrament that prepares one for the last moment, which wipes out the sins before death and disposes the soul to final union with God. I have in front of me a notice distributed to all the faithful in a Paris church to warn them of the date of the next Extreme Unction: "For those who are still active, the sacrament of the sick is celebrated in the presence of the whole Christian community during the Eucharistic celebration. Date: Sunday, at the 11 o'clock Mass." These anointings are invalid.

The same collectivist mentality has provoked the vogue of penitential celebrations. The sacrament of penance can only be of an individual nature. By definition and in conformity with its essence, it is, as I have previously pointed out, a judicial act, a judgment. A judgment cannot be made without having examined a cause; each one's case has to be heard in order to judge it and then to remit or to retain the sins. His Holiness John Paul II has insisted several times on this point, notably to the French bishops on April 1, 1982, telling them that personal confession followed by individual absolution is "a requirement of the dogmatic order." It is consequently impossible to justify these ceremonies of reconciliation by explaining that ecclesiastical discipline has become more relaxed, that it has adapted itself to the needs of the modern world. It is not a question of discipline. There was formerly one exception: general absolution given in a case of shipwreck, war, etc.; an absolution whose value is debated by learned writers. It is not permissible to make a rule out of the exception. If we consult the Acts of the Apostolic See we find the following expressions uttered both by Paul VI and John Paul II on various occasions: "the exceptional character of collective absolution," "in extraordinary situations of grave necessity," "quite exceptional nature."

Celebrations of this type have, however, become habitual though without becoming frequent in any one parish, due to the scarcity of faithful who are disposed to put themselves right with God more than two or three times a year. They no longer feel the need, as was quite foreseeable since the idea of sin has been wiped out of their minds. How many priests still remind people of the need for the sacrament of penance? One member of the faithful has told me that in going to confession in one or another of several Paris churches where he knows he will be able to find a "priest on duty," he often receives the congratulations or thanks of the priest, quite surprised to have a penitent.

These celebrations subjected to the creativity of the "animators" include singing, or else a record is played. Then comes the turn of the Liturgy of the word, followed by a litany-type of prayer to which the assembly responds, "Lord, have mercy upon me, a sinner," or else by a sort of general examination of conscience. The "I confess to Almighty God" precedes the absolution given once and for all to the whole congregation, which only leaves one problem: would a person present who did not want absolution receive it just the same? I see on a duplicated sheet distributed to those taking part in these ceremonies at Lourdes that the organizer has asked himself this question: "If we wish to receive absolution, let us dip our hands in the water and make the sign of the cross upon ourselves," and at the end, "Upon those who are marked by the sign of the cross with the water of the spring the priest lays his hands. Let us unite ourselves to his prayer and accept pardon from God."

The British Catholic paper, *The Universe*, a few years ago lent its support to a movement launched by two bishops which consisted of bringing back to the Church those of the faithful who had long since given up the practice of religion. The appeal made by the bishops resembled the public notices put out by families of runaway adolescents: "Little X, please come home. No one will grumble at you." It was then said to the future prodigal sons, "Your bishops invite you during this Lent to rejoice and celebrate. The Church offers to all her children, in the imitation of Christ, pardon for their sins, freely and without restriction, without their meriting it, and without their requesting it. She urges them to accept and begs them to return home. There are many who wish to return to the Church after years of separation but are unable to make up their minds to go to confession. At any rate, not straightaway . . ."

They could then accept the following offer: "At the Mission Mass which will be attended by the bishop in your deanery (here is given the time and the date) all those who are present are invited to accept the pardon of all their past sins. It is not necessary for them to go to confession at that moment. It will be sufficient for them to repent their sins and desire to return to God, and to confess their sins later, after having been again welcomed into the fold. Meanwhile they have only to let Our Father in heaven take them into His arms and embrace them tenderly. Subject to a generous act of repentance the bishop will grant to all those present and desiring it pardon for their sins. They may then immediately receive holy communion . . ."

The *Journal of the Grotto,* the bi-monthly magazine from Lourdes, reproducing this curious pastoral letter under the heading "General Absolution: Communion now, confession later," made the following comment: "Our readers will be fully aware of the deeply evangelical spirit which has inspired it, likewise the pastoral understanding of people's actual situation."

I do not know what results were obtained, but that is not the issue. Can pastoral needs take precedence over doctrine to the point of undertaking to give Communion in the Body of Christ indiscriminately to people who are probably in many cases in a state of mortal sin, after so many years without the practice of religion? Certainly not. How can we so lightly consider paying for the conversion with a sacrilege, and how much chance has this conversion of being followed by perseverance? We can observe, in any case, that before the council and before this "welcoming" pastoral method there were between fourteen and fifteen thousand conversions annually in England. They have dropped off to about five thousand. We recognize the tree by its fruit.

Catholics are just as confused in Great Britain as in France. If a sinner or an apostate, following his bishop's advice, presents himself for collective absolution and at the holy table in these conditions, does he not risk losing his confidence in the validity of sacraments so lightly accorded, when he has every reason to consider himself unworthy of them? What is going to happen if later on he neglects to "regularize" himself by going to confession? An unsuccessful return to the house of the Father will only make more difficult a final conversion.

That is what dogmatic laxity leads to. In the penitential ceremonies which take place, in a less extravagant manner, in our parishes, what certainty has the Catholic of being truly pardoned? He is given over to the same anxieties as Protestants, to interior torments provoked by doubt. He has certainly gained nothing by the change.

If it is a bad thing from the point of view of validity, it is also bad psychologically. For instance, how absurd to give collective absolution with the reservation that people with grave sins have to confess them personally immediately afterwards! People are not going to draw attention to themselves by showing that they have grave sins on their consciences, that is obvious! It is as though the secret of the confessional were violated.

We should add that the faithful who communicate after collective absolution will no longer see the need to present themselves before the judgment of penance, and that one can understand. The ceremonies of reconciliation are not complementary to auricular confession, they eliminate and supplant it. We are proceeding towards the disappearance of the Sacrament of Penance, established like the six others by Our Lord Himself. No pastoral concern can justify this.

For a sacrament to be valid, the *matter*, the *form* and the *intention* are all needed. The Pope himself cannot change that. The *matter* is of divine institution; the Pope cannot say "tomorrow we will use alcohol for the baptism of infants, or milk." Neither can he cange the essential of the *form*. There are essential words. For example, one cannot say, "I baptize thee in the name of God," because God Himself has settled this form: "Thou shalt baptize in the name of the Father, and of the Son and of the Holy Ghost."

The Sacrament of Confirmation has been equally maltreated. One formula current today is, "I sign thee with the Cross, and receive the Holy Spirit." But the minister does not then specify what is the special grace of the sacrament by which the Holy Ghost gives Himself, and the sacrament is invalid.

That is why I always respond to the requests of parents

who have doubts regarding the validity of the confirmation received by their children or who fear it will be administered invalidly, seeing what goes on around them. The cardinals to whom I had to explain myself in 1975 reproached me on this and since then similar reproaches are repeated through the press on all my journeys. I explained why I carried on in this way. I meet the wishes of the faithful who ask me for valid confirmation, even if it is not licit, because we are in a period when divine law, natural and supernatural, has precednece over positive ecclesiastical law when the latter opposes the former instead of being a channel to transmit it. We are passing through an extraordinary crisis and there need be no surprise if I sometimes adopt an attitude that is out of the ordinary.

The third condition of a valid sacrament is a right *intention*. The bishop or priest must have the intention of doing what the Church wills to be done. Not even the Pope can change that.

The priest's faith is not among the necessary elements. A priest or bishop may no longer have the faith; another may have it less; and another a faith that is not quite complete. That has no direct effect on the validity of the sacraments they administer, but may have an indirect one. One remembers Pope Leo XIII's decision that Anglican ordinations are invalid through a defect in the intention. Now it was because they had lost the faith, which is not only faith in God, but in all the truths contained in the Creed, including, "I believe in *one* holy Catholic and apostolic Church," that the Anglicans have not been able to do what the Church wills.

Are not priests who lose the faith in the same case? There are already priests who *no longer wish* to confect the Sacrament of the Eucharist according to the Council of Trent's definition. "No," they say, "the Council of Trent was a long time ago. Since then we have had Vatican II. Now it's trans-signification, or trans-finalization. Transubstantiation? The Real Presence of the Son of God under the appearances of bread and wine? Not in these days!"

When a priest talks like this, he makes no valid consecration. There is no Mass or Communion. For Christians are obliged to believe what the Council of Trent has defined about the Eucharist until the end of time. One can make the terms of a dogma clearer, but not change them; that is impossible. Vatican II did not add anything or retract anything; and it could not have done so. Anyone who declares that he does not accept transubstantiation is, in the terms of the Council of Trent, *anathema,* that is, cut off from the Church.

This is why Catholics in this latter part of the twentieth century have a duty to be more vigilant than their fathers were. They must not let just any idea be imposed upon them, in the name of the new theology or the new religion: for what this new religion wants is not what the Church wills.

VII
The New Priests

To the man in the street, even the most indifferent to religious questions, it is obvious that there are fewer and fewer priests, and the newspapers regularly remind him of the fact. It is over fifteen years ago since the book appeared with the title "Tomorrow a Church without Priests?"

Yet the situation is even more serious than it appears. The question has also to be asked, how many priests still have the faith? And even a further question, regarding some of the priests ordained in recent years: are they true priests at all? Put it another way, are their ordinations valid? The same doubt overhangs other sacraments. It applies to certain ordinations of bishops such as that which took place in Brussels in the summer of 1982 when the consecrating bishop said to the ordinand "Be an apostle like Gandhi, Helder Camara, and Mohamed!" Can we reconcile these references, at least as regards Gandhi and Mohamed, with the evident intention of doing what the Church intends?

Here is the order of service for a priestly ordination which took place at Toulouse a few years ago. A commentator starts off, introducing the ordinand by his christian-name C., with the words "He has decided to live more thoroughly his self-dedication to God and to man by consecrating himself entirely to the service of the Church in the working-class." C. has worked out his "pathway," that is to say, his seminary training, in a team. It is this team who present him to the bishop: "We request you to recognize and authenticate his application and ordain him priest."

The bishop then asks him several questions purporting to be a definition of the priesthood: Do you wish to be ordained a priest, "to be, with the believers, a Sign and a Witness of what Mankind is seeking, in its striving for Justice, for Brotherhood and for Peace," "to serve the people of God," "to recognize in men's lives, the action of God in the ways they take, in their cultural patterns, in the choices open to them," "to celebrate the action of Christ and perform this service;" do you wish "to share with me and with the body of bishops the responsibility that has been entrusted to us for the service of the Gospel?"

The "matter" of the sacrament has been preserved in the laying on of hands which takes place next, and likewise the "form," namely the words of ordination. But we are obliged to point out that the intention is far from clear. Has the priest been ordained for the exclusive service of one social class and, first and foremost, to establish justice, fellowship and peace at a level which appears to be limited to the natural order only? The eucharistic celebration which follows, "the first Mass" in effect, of the new priest was, in fact, on these lines. The offertory has been specially composed for the circumstances. "We welcome you, Lord, by receiving on your behalf this bread and wine which you offer us; we wish to show by this all our work and our efforts to build a more just and more humane world, all that we are trying to bring about so that better living conditions may follow . . ." The prayer over the offerings is even more dubious: "Look, Lord we offer you this bread and this wine, that they may become for us *one of the ways in which you are present.*" No! People who celebrate in this manner do not believe in the Real Presence!

One thing is certain; the first victim of this scandalous ordination is the young man who had just pledged himself for ever without exactly knowing to what, or thinking that he knows. How can he not fail, sooner or later, to ask himself certain questions? Because the ideal that has been proposed to him cannot satisfy him for long; the ambiguity of his mission will become evident. The priest is essentially a man of faith. If he no longer knows what he is, he loses faith in himself, and in his priesthood.

The definition of the priesthood given by Saint Paul and by the Council of Trent has been radically altered. The priest is no longer one who goes up to the altar and offers up to God a sacrifice of praise, for the remission of sins. The relative order of purposes has been inverted. The priesthood has a first aim, which is to offer the sacrifice; that of evangelization is secondary.

The case of C., which is far from being unique, as we know of many examples, shows to what extent evangelization has taken precedence over the sacrifice and the sacraments. It has become an end in itself. This grave error has had serious consequences.

Evangelization, deprived of its aim, loses direction and seeks purposes that are pleasing to the world, such as a false "social justice" and a false "liberty." These acquire new names: development, progress, building up the world, improving living-conditions, pacifism. Here is the sort of language which has led to all the revolutions.

The sacrifice of the altar being no longer the first purpose of the priesthood, it is the whole of the sacraments which are at stake and for which the "person responsible for the parish sector" and his "team" will call upon the laity, who are themselves overburdened with trade unions or political tasks, often more political than trade unions. In fact, the priests who engage in social struggles choose almost exclusively the most politicized organizations. Within these they fight against political, ecclesiastical, family and social structures. Nothing can remain. Communism has found no agents more effective than these priests.

I was explaining one day to a Cardinal what I was doing in my seminaries, with their spirituality directed above all to the deepening of the theology of the Sacrifice of the Mass and towards liturgical prayer. He said to me, "But Monsignor, that is exactly the opposite of what our young priests now want. We now define the priest only in terms of evangelization." I replied, "What evangelization? If it does not have a fundamental and essential relationship with the Holy Sacrifice, how do you understand it? A political evangelization, or social, or humanitarian?"

If he no longer announces Jesus Christ, the apostle becomes a militant and marxist trade unionist. That is very natural. We quite understand it. He needs a new *mystique* and he finds it this way; but loses that of the altar. We must not be surprised that, completely bewildered, he gets married and abandons the priesthood. In France, in 1970, 285 ordinations; in 1980, 111. And how many of them have returned or will return to civil life? Even the startling figures we have quoted do not correspond to the actual decline in numbers of the clergy. What is offered to young men and what it is said they "now desire" evidently does not satisfy their aspirations.

The proof is easy to demonstrate. There are no more vocations because they no longer know what is the Sacrifice of the Mass. In consequence, one can no longer define what the priest is. On the other hand, where the Sacrifice is known and respected as the Church has always taught, vocations are plentiful.

I have witnessed this in my own seminaries. All we do is to affirm the everlasting truths. Vocations have come to us of their own accord, without publicizing. The only advertizing has been done by the modernists. I have ordained 187 priests in thirteen years. Since 1983 the regular numbers are from 35 to 40 ordinations per year. The young men who apply to enter Ecône, Ridgefield (USA), Zaitzkofen (West Germany), Francisco Alvarez (Argentina) and Albano (Italy) are drawn by the Sacrifice of the Mass.

What an extraordinary grace for a young man to go up to the altar as the minister of Our Lord, to be another Christ! Nothing is finer or greater here on earth. It is worth the cost of leaving one's family, of giving up having a family, or renouncing the world and accepting poverty.

But if there is no longer that attraction, then I say frankly, it is not worthwhile, and that is why the seminaries are empty.

Let them continue on the lines adopted by the Church for the last 20 years, and to the question "Will there still be priests in the year 2000?" The answer must be, "No." But if there is a return to the true notions of the Faith, there will be vocations, both for seminaries and for the religious orders.

For what is it that makes the greatness and the beauty of a priest or a nun? It is the offering up of oneself as a victim at the altar with Our Lord Jesus Christ. Otherwise the religious life is meaningless. The young men are just as generous in our times as they were in former times. They long to make an offering of themselves. It is our times that are defective.

Everything is bound up together. By attacking the base of the building it is destroyed entirely. No more Mass, no more priests. The ritual, before it was altered, had the bishop say "Receive the power to offer to God the Holy Sacrifice and to celebrate Holy Mass both for the living and for the dead, in the name of the Lord." He had previously blessed the hands of the ordinand by pronouncing these words "So that all that they bless may be blessed and all that they consecrate may be consecrated and sanctified." The power conferred is expressed without ambiguity: "That for the salvation of Thy people and by their holy blessing, they may effect the Transubstantiation of the bread and the wine into the Body and Blood of thy Divine Son."

Nowadays the bishop says, "Receive the offering of the holy people to present it to God." He makes the new priest an intermediary rather than the holder of the ministerial priesthood and the offerer of a sacrifice. The conception is wholly different. The priest has always been considered in Holy Church as someone having a character conferred by the Sacrament of Order. Yet we have seen a bishop, not "suspended," write, "The priest is not somebody who does things that the ordinary faithful don't do; he is not 'another Christ', any more than any other baptized person." This bishop was merely drawing the conclusions from the teaching that has prevailed since the Council and the liturgy.

A confusion has been made with regard to the relation of the priesthood of the faithful and that of priests. Now as the cardinals said who were appointed to make their observations on the infamous Dutch catechism, "the greatness of the ministerial priesthood (that of priests) in its participation in the priesthood of Christ, differs from the common priesthood of the faithful in a manner that is not only of degree but also of essence." To maintain the contrary, on this point alone, is to align oneself with Protestantism.

The unchanging doctrine of the Church is that the priest is invested with a sacred and indelible character. *"Tu es sacerdos in aeternum."* Whatever he may do, before the angels, before God, in all eternity, he will remain a priest. Even if he throws away his cassock, wears a red pullover or any other color or commits the most awful crimes, it will not alter things. The Sacrament of Orders has made a change in his nature.

We are far from the priest "chosen by the assembly to fulfill a function in the Church" and still more so from the priest for a limited period, suggested by some, at the end of which the official for worship — for I can think of no other term to describe him — would take his place again amongst the faithful.

This desacralized view of the priestly ministry leads quite naturally to querying priestly celibacy. There are noisy pressure groups calling for its abolition in spite of the repeated warnings of the Roman magisterium. We have seen in Holland, seminarians go on strike against ordinations to obtain "guarantees" in this matter. I shall not quote the names of those bishops who have got up to urge the Holy See to reconsider the subject.

The subject would not even arise if the clergy had kept the right understanding of the Mass and of the priesthood. For the true reason appears of itself when we fully understand these two realities. It is the same reason for which Our Blessed Lady remained a virgin: having borne Our Lord within her womb it was perfectly right and fitting that she should remain so. Likewise, the priest by the words he pronounces at the Consecration, brings down God upon earth. He has such a closeness with God, a spiritual being, spirit above all, that it is right, just and eminently fitting that he also should be a virgin and remain celibate.

But, some object, there are married priests in the East. However, let us not deceive ourselves: it is only toleration. The eastern bishop may not marry, not those holding important positions. This clergy respects priestly celibacy, which forms part of the most ancient Tradition of the Church and which the apostles had observed from the moment of Pentecost. Those who like Saint Peter were already married continued to live with their wives, but "knew" them no longer.

It is noticeable that the priests who succomb to the mirage of a so-called social or political mission almost automatically get married. The two things go together.

People would have us believe that the present times justify all sorts of licence, that it is impossible under present day conditions to live a chaste life, that the vows of virginity for religious people are an anachronism. The experience of the last twenty years shows that the attacks made on the priesthood under the pretext of adapting it to the present time are fatal to it. Yet a "Church without priests" is not to be envisaged because the Church is essentially sacerdotal.

In these sad times they want free-love for the laity and marriage for the clergy. If you perceive in this apparent illogicality an implacable logic having as its objective the ruin of Christian society, you are seeing things as they are and your assessment is correct.

VIII
The New Catechisms

Among Catholics, I have often heard, and continue to hear the remark, "They want to impose a new religion on us." Is this an exaggeration? The modernists, who have infiltrated themselves everywhere in the Church and lead the dance, sought at first to reassure us: "Oh no, you have got the impression because old obsolete ways have been changed, for compelling reasons: we cannot pray now exactly as people used to pray, we have had to sweep away the dust, adopt a language that can be understood by our contemporaries and open ourselves up to our separated brethren . . . but nothing is changed, of course."

Then they began to take fewer precautions, and the bolder ones among them began to make admissions, in little groups of like-minded people and even publicly. One Father Cardonnel went round preaching a new Christianity in which "that precious transcendence that makes God into a Universal Monarch" would be challenged. He openly adopted Loisy's modernism: "If you were born into a Christian family, the catechisms you learnt are mere skeletons of the faith." And, "Our Christianity would seem to be neo-Capitalist at best." And Cardinal Suenens, after reconstructing the Church to his own liking, called for "an opening up to the widest theological pluralism" and for the setting up of a hierarchy of truths, with some that must be strongly believed, others that must be believed a little, and others of no importance.

In 1973, on the premises of the Archbishop's house at Paris, Fr. Bernard Feillet gave a course of lectures of a thoroughly official kind, under the banner of "Adult Christian Formation." In it he repeatedly affirmed, "Christ did not conquer death. He was put to death by death. On the level of life, Christ was conquered, and we shall all be conquered: the fact is that faith is not justified by anything; it must be a cry of protest against the universe which ends, as we said just now, in the perception of absurdity, in the consciousness of damnation, and in the reality of nothingness."

I could quote an impressive number of cases of this kind, which caused various degrees of scandal and were repudiated more or less—some of them not at all. But it passed over the heads of the Catholic people as a whole. If they learnt of these things in the newspapers they thought of them as abuses that were exceptional and did not affect their own faith. But they began to be worried when they found in their children's hands catechisms which no longer set out Catholic doctrine as it had been taught from time immemorial.

All the new catechisms that draw their inspiration to a greater or less degree from the *Dutch Catechism* published in 1966 were so spurious that the Pope appointed a commission of cardinals to examine it. They met in April 1967 at Gazzada in Lombardy. Now this commission raised ten points regarding which it advised the Holy See to demand modifications. It was a way of saying, in conformity with the post-conciliar style, that on these points there was disagreement with the teaching of the Church. A few years earlier they would have been forthrighty condemned and the Dutch Catechism put on the Index. The errors or omissions concerned did, in fact, touch upon essentials of the faith.

What do we find in it? The Dutch Catechism ignores the angels, and does not treat human souls as being directly created by God. It insinuates that original sin was not transmitted by our first parents to all their descendants but is contracted by men through their living in the human community, where evil reigns, as though it were a sort of epidemic. There is no affirmation of the virginity of Mary. Nor does it say that Our Lord died for our sins, being sent for this purpose by His Father, and that this was the price by which divine Grace was restored to us. Consequently, the Mass is presented not as a sacrifice but as a banquet. Neither the Real Presence or the reality of Transubstantiation are clearly affirmed.

The Church's infallibility and the fact that she is the possessor of the truth have vanished from this teaching, likewise the possibility for the human intellect to "declare and attain to revealed mysteries:" thereby one arrives at agnosticism and relativism. The ministerial priesthood is minimised. The office of the bishops is considered as a mandate entrusted to them by the "people of God," and their teaching authority is seen as a sanctioning of the belief held by the community of the faithful. And the Pope no longer has his full, supreme and universal authority.

Neither is the Holy Trinity, the mystery of the three divine Persons, presented in a satisfactory manner. The commission also criticized the explanation given of the efficacity of the sacraments, of the definition of a miracle, and of the fate of the souls of the just after death. It found a great deal of vagueness in the exposition of the laws of morality, and the "solutions to cases of conscience" put a low price of the indissolubility of marriage.

Even if all the rest of the book is "good and praise-worthy"—which is not surprising, since Modernists, as St. Pius X firmly pointed out, have always mixed truth and falsehood together—nevertheless, we have seen enough to be able to describe it as a perverse production particularly dangerous to faith. Yet without waiting for the commission's report, on the contrary going full tilt ahead, the promoters of the operation had the book published in several languages. And the text has never since been altered. Sometimes the commission's statement is annexed to the list of contents, sometimes not. I shall refer later on to the problem of obedience. Who is being disobedient in this affair? And who denounces this "catechism"?

The Dutch set the pace. We have quickly caught them

up. I shall not relate the history of the French catechism, but will pause to consider its latest manifestation, the "Catholic collection of key documents of the Faith" entitled *Pierres Vivantes* (*Living Stones*), and the accompanying flood of "catechetical studies." These works ought, out of respect for the word "catechesis" used in all of them, to proceed on a question-and-answer method. However, they have abandoned this form, which allowed the content of the faith to be studied systematically, and they hardly ever give answers. *Pierres Vivantes* avoids affirming anything, except new and unusual propositions that have nothing to do with Tradition.

When dogmas are mentioned, they are spoken of as the particular beliefs of a section of mankind which this book calls "the Christians," putting them on a level with the Jews, the Protestants, the Buddhists, and even the agnostics and atheists. In several courses the catechists are invited to ask the child to choose a religion, no matter which. It will also be for his good to listen to unbelievers, who have much to teach him. What matters is to "belong to the team," to help one another as class-mates and to prepare for the social struggles of tomorrow in which one will have to take part, even alongside communists, as is seen in the edifying story of Madeleine Delbrel. Her story is sketched in *Pierres Vivantes* and told at length in other courses. Another "saint" put forward as an example to children is Martin Luther King, while Marx and Proudhon are vaunted as "great defenders of the working class" who "appear to come from outside the Church." The Church, you see, would have liked to have taken up this fight, but did not know how to set about it. She contented herself with "denouncing injustice." This is what children are being taught.

But still more serious is the discredit that is being cast upon the Scriptures, the work of the Holy Ghost. Whereas one would have expected to see the selection of Biblical texts begin with the creation of the world and of man, *Pierres Vivantes* begins with the book of Exodus, under the title of "God creates His people." Catholics must surely be not only confused but disconcerted and disgusted by such a misuse of words.

We have to arrive at the First Book of Samuel before returning to Genesis to learn that God did *not* create the world. I am not inventing anything here, either. We read: "The author of the story of creation, like many people, is wondering how the world began. Believers have given thought to it. One of them wrote a poem...." Then, at the court of Solomon, other wise men reflected on the problem of evil. To explain it they wrote a "picture-story," and we have the temptation by the serpent and the fall of Adam and Eve. But not the chastisement. The story is cut at that point. God does not punish, just as the Church no longer condemns, except those who stay faithful to Tradition. Orignal sin (printed between quotation marks) is "an illness from birth," "an infirmity going back to the origins of humanity," something very vague and inexplicable.

Of course, the whole of religion crumbles. If we can no longer give an explanation of the problem of evil, there is no further point in preaching, saying Mass or hearing confessions. Who will listen to us?

The New Testament opens with Pentecost. The emphasis is laid on that first community uttering its cry of faith. Next, these Christians "remember," and the story of Our Lord emerges little by little from the clouds of their memory, beginning with the end: the Last Supper, or Calvary. Then comes the public life, and finally the infancy under the ambiguous heading "The first disciples tell the story of Jesus' childhood."

On such foundations these courses have no difficulty in giving the impression that the Gospel accounts of the infancy of Christ are pious legends of the sort that ancient peoples were accustomed to invent when they recorded the lives of their great men. *Pierres Vivantes* also gives a late dating of the Gospels which diminishes their credibility and tendentiously portrays the Apostles and their successors as preaching, celebrating the Mysteries and teaching before "presenting their own reading of the life of Jesus on the ba-

sis of their experience." The facts are turned upside down:
the Apostles' personal experience becomes the origin of
revelation, instead of the revelation shaping their thought
and their lives.

When it comes to the "four last things," *Pierres Vivantes*
is confusing and disquieting. What is the soul? Reply: "We
need breath if we are to run; when someone dies, we say
'he has breathed his last'. The breath is the life, the intimate
life of a person. We also say, 'the soul'." In another chapter
the soul is likened to the heart, the heart which beats, and
loves. The heart is also the seat of the conscience. What can
we make of this? And death: what is that? The authors
come to no conclusion. "For some, death is the final ceasing
of life. Others think we can live after death, but do not
know for sure. Finally there are others who have a firm assurance about this: Christians are among them." It is up to
the child to choose: death is a matter of opinion. But is not
the one who is being taught the Catechism a Christian? In
that case, why speak to him of Christians in the third person instead of stating firmly, "We Christians know that
eternal life exists and that the soul does not die?"

Paradise also is a subject treated equivocally: "Christians sometimes speak of Paradise to describe the perfect
joy of being with God for ever after death; it is Heaven, the
Kingdom of God, Eternal Life, the Reign of Peace." This is a
very hypothetical explanation. It would seem that one is
dealing with a figure of speech, a reassuring metaphor used
by Christians. But Our Lord has promised us Heaven, if we
keep His commandments; and the Church has always defined that as "a place of perfect happiness where the angels
and the elect see God and possess Him for ever." This
catechesis shows a definite going-back on what the catechisms used to affirm. The only result will be a lack of confidence in the truths taught and in a spiritual disarmament:
what is the good of resisting our instincts and following the
narrow way if we are not very sure of what awaits a Christian after death?

A Catholic does not go to the priests or his bishop asking for suggestions to enable him to form his own idea about God, or the world, or the last things. He asks them what he must believe and what he must do. If they reply with a whole range of propositions and patterns for living, then it only remains for him to make up his own personal religion: he becomes a protestant. This catechesis is turning children into little protestants.

The keynote of the reform is the drive against certainties. Catholics who have them are branded as misers guarding their treasures, as greedy egotists who should be ashamed of themselves. The important thing is to be open to contrary opinions, to admit diversity, to respect the ideas of freemasons, marxists, muslims, even animists. The mark of a holy life is to join in dialogue with error.

Thenceforth everything is permitted. I have already spoken of the consequences of the new definition of marriage. These are not the remote consequences which would follow if Christians took this definition literally: on the contrary, they have not been slow to appear, as we can judge by the moral permissiveness which is becoming daily more widespread. But what is still more shocking is that the catechesis is aiding this process. Let us take an example from some "catechetical material" as they call it, published with the episcopal *imprimatur* about 1972 at Lyons, and intended for teachers. The title: "Behold the Man." In the section dealing with morals we read: "Jesus did not intend to leave to posterity a moral system, either political, sexual, or what you will. His only permanent insistence is love for one another. Beyond that, you are free; it is for you to choose what in every instance is the best way to express this love which you bear to your fellow-men."

The section on "purity" draws consequences from this general principle. After explaining, at the expense of the book of Genesis, that clothing only appeared later "as a sign of social rank or dignity" and to serve "a purpose of dissimulation," purity is defined as follows. "To be pure is to be in order, to be faithful to nature ...To be pure means being in harmony, at peace with men and with the earth; it means being in accord with the great forces of nature without either resistance or violence." Next we find a question and an answer: "Is a purity of this sort compatible with the purity of Christians? —Not only is it compatible, it is necessary to a truly human and Christian purity. Jesus Christ neither denied or rejected any of the discoveries and acquisitions that are the fruit of the long searching of the peoples. Quite the contrary; He came to give them an extraordinary extension: 'I came not to destroy but to fulfill'."

In support of their claims the authors give the example of Mary Magdalen: "In that gathering it is she who is pure, because she has loved much, loved deeply." This is their manner of falsifying the Gospel: of Mary Magdalen they retain only the sin, the dissolute life. The pardon that Our Lord granted her is presented as an approval of her past, and no notice is taken of the exhortation "Go, and sin no more," nor the firm resolution that led the former sinner to Calvary, faithful to her Master for the rest of her days. This revolting book knows no limits: "Can one have relations with a girl," the authors ask, "even if one knows that it is for pleasure or to see what a woman is like?" And they reply "To put the problem of the laws of purity in this way is unworthy of a true man, a loving man, a Christian. Would not that mean imposing a strait-jacket, an intolerable yoke? When Christ came precisely to free us from the heavy burdens of laws: 'My yoke is easy and My burden light'." You see how the holiest words are interpreted so as to pervert souls! From Saint Augustine they have remembered only one sentence, "Love, and do as you will!"

I have been sent some contemptible books published in Canada. They speak only of sex and always in capital letters: "sexuality lived in faith," "sexual promotion," etc. These pictures are absolutely disgusting. It seems that they wish at all costs to give children a desire for and an obsession with sex; to make them think it is the only thing in life. Many Christian parents have protested, but nothing has been done about it, for a good reason: on the back page we read that these catechisms have been approved by the

Catechetical Commission. The permission to print has been given by the President of the Episcopal Commission for Religious Teaching of Quebec!

Another catechism approved by the Canadian episcopate calls upon children to break with everything—so as to re-discover their personality that all these ties have smothered, and free themselves from the complexes that come from society or from the family. Always looking for justification in the Gospel, those who give this sort of advice claim that Christ made similar breaks and thereby revealed Himself to be the Son of God. So it is His wish that we should do likewise.

How can one accept an idea so contrary to the Catholic religion on the pretext that it is covered by episcopal authority? Instead of talking about breaks we need to cherish the bonds that make up our life. What is the love of God if not a link with God and obedience to Him and His commandments? And the bond with our parents, our love for them, is a bond for life, not of death. But they are now presented to children as something constraining and repressing which diminishes their personality, and from which they must free themselves!

No, there can be no question of your allowing your children to be corrupted in this manner. I say frankly, you cannot send them to these catechism classes that make them lose their faith.

IX
The New Theology

The ravages caused by the new catechism are already visible in the generation which has been exposed to it. As required by the Sacred Congregation for Seminaries and Universities since 1970, I had included in the plan of studies for my seminaries one year's spirituality at the beginning of the course. Spirituality includes the study of asceticism, mysticism, training in meditation and prayer, deepening the notions of virtue, supernatural grace, the presence of the Holy Ghost. Very soon we had to think again. We realized that these young men, who had come with a strong desire to become true priests, and having an interior life deeper than many of their contemporaries, and accustomed to prayer, were lacking the fundamental ideas of our Faith. They had never learned them. During the year of spirituality, we had to teach them the catechism!

I have many times told the story of the birth of Ecône. In this house situated in the Valais in Switzerland, between Sion and Martigny, it was originally intended that the future priests would complete only their first year (of spirituality). Then they would follow the university course at Fribourg. A complete seminary (at Ecône) took shape as soon as it did because the University at Fribourg could not provide a truly Catholic education. The Church has always considered the university chairs of theology, canon law, liturgy and Church law as organs of her magisterium or at least of her preaching. Now it is quite certain that at present in all, or nearly all of the Catholic universities, the orthodox Catholic faith is no longer being taught. I have not found one doing so, either in free Europe, or in the United States, or in South America. There are always some professors who, under the pretext of theological research, express opinions which are contradictory to our faith, and not only on points of secondary importance.

I have already spoken of the Dean of the Faculty of Theology at Strasbourg, for whom the presence of Our Lord in the Mass can be compared to that of Wagner at the Bayreuth Festival. It is no longer a question of the Novus Ordo for him. The world is evolving so rapidly that these things are quickly left behind. He considers that we must foresee a Eucharist which will emerge from the group itself. What does he mean by this? He is not sure himself. But in his book, *Contemporary Thought and Expression of Eucharistic Faith*, he prophesies that members of that group gathered together will create the feeling of communion in Christ who will be present amongst them, but above all under the species of bread and wine. He scoffs at calling the Eucharist "an efficacious sign" (a definition common to all the sacraments). "That is ridiculous," he says; "we can no longer say that sort of thing; in our day it no longer makes sense."

The young students who hear these things from their professors and moreover from the dean of the faculty, and young seminarists who attend the classes, are little by little infected with the error. They receive a training which is no longer Catholic. It is the same for those who not long ago heard a Dominican professor at Fribourg assuring them that premarital relations are both normal and desirable.

My own seminarians knew another Dominican who taught them to compose new versions of the Canon of the Mass. "It isn't difficult; here are a few principles you can easily use when you are priests." We could go on with examples like this. Smulders, at the Theological Faculty in Amsterdam, suspects that St. Paul and St. John invented the concept of Jesus as Son of God, and thus he rejects the dogma of the Incarnation. Schillebeeckx, at the University of Nimjaegen, comes out with the most outrageous ideas; he has invented "trans-signification," subjecting the dogma (of transubstantiation) to the conditions of each period of history; and he assigns a social and temporal definition to the doctrine of salvation. Küng, at Tübingen, before he was forbidden to teach in a chair of *Catholic* theology, questioned the mystery of the Blessed Trinity, of the Virgin Mary, and the sacraments, and described Jesus as a public story-teller lacking"all theological training." Snackenburg, at the University of Würtzburg, accuses St. Matthew of having forged the confession, "Thou art the Christ," in order to authenticate the primacy of Peter. Rahner, who died recently, minimized Tradition in his lectures at the University of Münich, virtually denying the Incarnation by always speaking of Our Lord as a man "naturally conceived," denying original sin and the Immaculate Conception and recommending theological plurality.

All these people are praised to the skies by the leading spokesmen of neo-modernism. They have the support of the press, in such a way that their theories assume importance in the eyes of the public and their names are known to all. They thus appear to represent the entirety of theology and gain support for the idea that the Church has changed. They have been able to continue their subversive teaching for many years, interrupted sometimes by mild sanctions. The popes issue regular reminders of the limits of the theologian's competence. Pope John Paul II said quite recently, "It is not possible to turn away and detach oneself from those fundamental reference points, the defined dogmas, without losing one's Catholic identity." Schillebeeckx, Küng and Pohier have been reprimanded but have not suffered sanctions, the last-named for a book in which he denies the bodily resurrection of Christ. And who would have imagined that at the Roman Universities, including the Gregorian, under the pretext of theological research the most incredible theories are allowed, regarding the relationship of Church and State, divorce, and other fundamental questions?

There is no doubt that abolishing the Holy Office, which had always been seen by the Church as the tribunal of the

Faith, has favored these abuses. Until then anyone—layman, priest or *a fortiori* a bishop—could submit to the Holy Office any text, any article and ask whether the Church thought the writing was in conformity or not with the Catholic doctrine. A month or six weeks later, the Holy Office would reply: "This is correct, this is false, that must be made clear; one part is true and one part false . . ."

Every document was thus examined and judged definitively. Does it shock you to learn that the writings of another person could be submitted to a tribunal? But what happens in civil society? Is there not a Constitutional Council to decide what is and what is not in conformity with the Constitution? Are there not tribunals to deal with cases affecting private individuals and groups? We can even ask a judge to intervene in cases of public morality, against an offensive poster or against a magazine sold openly, if the cover consititutes an outrage against public morals, although the limits of what is permitted have widened considerably in recent times in many countries.

But in the Church, a tribunal was no longer acceptable; we could no longer judge or condemn. The modernists, like the Protestants, have singled out from the gospels their favorite phrase "Thou shalt not judge." But they ignore the fact that immediately after, Our Lord said: "Beware of false prophets . . . by their fruits you shall know them." A Catholic must not make ill-considered judgments on the faults and personal actions of his brethren, but Christ has commanded him to preserve his faith, and how can he do this without casting a critical eye upon what he is given to read or to hear? Any dubious opinion could be submitted to the magisterium; that was the purpose of the Holy Office. But since the reform, the Holy Office has defined itself as "the Office for Theological Research." A considerable difference.

I remember asking Cardinal Browne, former Superior General of the Dominicans, who had long been at the Holy Office, "Your Eminence, do you have the impression that this is a radical change, or merely superficial and outward?" "Oh no," he replied, "the change is fundamental".

This is why we must not be surprised if little or nothing is condemned, if the Tribunal for the Faith of the Church no longer fulfills its duty toward theologians and all those who write on religious topics. It follows from this that errors are everywhere. They spread from the university chairs to the catechisms and to the remotest parish presbyteries. The poison of heresy ends by contaminating the whole Church. The ecclesiastical magisterium is in a very serious crisis.

The most absurd reasoning is used to support the activity of these *soit disant* theologians. We have seen a certain Father Duquoc, professor at Lyons, travelling all over France giving lectures on the advisibillity of conferring temporary priesthood on certain of the faithful, including women. A good number of the faithful have protested here and there, and one bishop in the South of France has taken a firm stand against this controversial preacher. This happens occasionally. But at Laval the scandalized laity received this reply from their bishop: "It is our absolute duty in this case to preserve freedom of speech within the Church." This is astonishing. Where did he get this idea of freedom of speech? It is completely alien to the law of the Church; yet he considers the defence of it to be a bishop's absolute duty! It amounts to a complete inversion of episcopal responsibility, which should consist of defending the Faith and preserving the people entrusted to him from heresy.

It is necessary to cite examples from the public sphere. I would ask the reader to believe that I am not writing this book to criticize personalities. That, too, was always the attitude of the Holy Office. It did not examine persons, but only writings. A theologian might complain that they had condemned one of his books without giving him a hearing. But precisely—the Holy Office condemned particular writings and not authors. It would say, "This book contains statements which are at variance with the traditional doctrine of the Church." Just that! Why go back to the person who had written them? His intentions and his culpability are the concern of another tribunal, that of penance.

X
Ecumenism

In this confusion of ideas (in which some Catholics now seem to be quite at ease), there is a tendency especially dangerous to the Faith, the more so because it masquerades as charity. The word which appeared in 1927 during a congress held at Lausanne, Switzerland, would have put Catholics on their guard if they had consulted their dictionaries. "Ecumenism: a movement toward reunion of all Christian churches in a single church." Now it is clear that we cannot combine contradictory principles. We cannot unite truth and error so as to form one thing, except by adopting the error and rejecting all or part of the truth. Ecumenism is self-condemnatory.

The expression has become so fashionable since the last Council that it has slipped into everyday speech. We speak of universal ecumenism, of exploratory ecumenism and whatever else, to express a taste or a preference for diversity and eclecticism.

In religious language ecumenism has recently been extended to non-Christian religions and translated straightway into action. A newspaper in western France gives us a perfect example of the way this evolutionary process works. In a small parish near Cherbourg, the Catholic population showed concern for the welfare of the Muslim workers who had arrived to work on a building site. For this charitable action they can only be praised. In the next stage, however, the Muslims asked for a place to celebrate the fast of Ramadan, and the Christians offered them the basement of their church. Then a Koranic school opened. After a couple

of years the Christians invited the Muslims to celebrate
Christmas with them "around a common prayer made up
of extracts from the Koran and verses from the Gospels."
Misplaced charity had led these Christians to come to terms
with error.

In Lille the Dominicans have offered the Muslims a
chapel to be turned into a mosque. In Versailles collections
have been taken up in the churches for the "purchase of a
place of worship for the Muslims." Two other chapels have
been handed over, at Roubaix and at Marseilles, together
with a church at Argenteuil. Catholics have become the
worst enemy of the Church of Christ—which is what Islam
is—and are offering their money to Mohammed. It appears
that there are more than four hundred mosques in France,
and in many cases Catholics have given the money for their
construction.

Nowadays all religions have the Freedom of the City
within the Church. A French cardinal celebrated Mass in
the presence of some Tibetan monks, dressed in their cere-
monial robes and seated in the front row, bowing before
them while a commentator announced: "The bonzes share
with us in the Eucharistic celebration." In a church at Ren-
nes, worship of Buddha was celebrated. In Italy, twenty
monks were solemnly initiated into Zen by a Buddhist.

I could cite endless examples of such syncretism going
on around us. We see associations developing, movements
being born which always seem to find an ecclesiastic as
leader who wants to join in the quest to "blend all spiritu-
alities in love." Or astounding projects like the transformation of Notre Dame de la Garde (at Marseilles) into a place
of monotheistic worship for Christians, Muslims and Jews,
a project which fortunately was stopped by some groups of
lay people.

Ecumenism in the strict sense, i.e., as practised among
Christians, has motivated joint Eucharistic celebrations with
Protestants, such as at Strasbourg. The Anglicans were invited to Chartres Cathedral to celebrate "Eucharistic Communion." The only celebration which is not allowed, either

at Chartres, or at Strasbourg, or at Marseilles, is that of Holy Mass according to the rite codified by Saint Pius V.

What conclusion can be drawn from all this by a Catholic who sees Church authorities condoning such scandalous ceremonies? If all religions are of equal value, he could very well work out his salvation with Buddhists or Protestants. He is running the risk of losing faith in the true Church. This in fact is what is suggested to him. They want to submit the Church to natural law; they want to put it on the same footing with other religions. They refuse to say—even priests, seminarists and seminary professors—that the Catholic Church is the only Church, that she possesses the truth, that she alone is able to lead men to salvation through Jesus Christ. "The Church is only a spiritual leaven within society, but the same as other religions; a bit more than the others, perhaps . . ." They sometimes grant it a slight superiority, if you press them.

If this is the case, then the Church is merely useful; she is no longer indispensible. She is only one of the means of salvation.

We must say it clearly: such a concept is radically opposed to Catholic dogma. The Church is the one ark of salvation, and we must not be afraid to affirm it. You have often heard it said, "Outside the Church there is no salvation"—a dictum which offends contemporary minds. It is easy to believe that this doctrine is no longer in effect, that it has been dropped. It seems excessively severe.

Yet nothing, in fact, has changed; nothing can be changed in this area. Our Lord did not found a number of churches: He founded only One. There is only one Cross by which we can be saved, and that Cross has been given to the Catholic Church. It has not been given to others. To His Church, His mystical bride, Christ has given all graces. No grace in the world, no grace in the history of humanity is distributed except through her.

Does that mean that no Protestant, no Muslim, no Buddhist or animist will be saved? No, it would be a second error to think that. Those who cry for intolerance in interpreting St. Cyprian's formula, "Outside the Church there is no salvation," also reject the Creed, "I confess one baptism for the remission of sins", and are insufficiently instructed as to what baptism is. There are three ways of receiving it: the baptism of water; the baptism of blood (that of the martyrs who confessed the faith while still catechumens) and baptism of desire.

Baptism of desire can be *explicit*. Many times in Africa I heard one of our catechumens say to me, "Father, baptize me straightaway because if I die before you come again, I shall go to hell." I told him,"No, if you have no mortal sin on your conscience and if you desire baptism, then you already have the grace in you".

The doctrine of the Church also recognizes *implicit*—baptism of desire. This consists in doing the will of God. God knows all men and He knows that amongst Protestants, Muslims, Buddhists and in the whole of humanity there are men of good will. They receive the grace of baptism without knowing it, but in an effective way. In this way they become part of the Church.

The error consists in thinking that they are saved by their religion. They are saved in their religion but not by it. There is no Buddhist church in heaven, no Protestant church. This is perhaps hard to accept, but it is the truth. I did not found the Church, but rather Our Lord the Son of God. As priests we must state the truth.

But at the cost of what difficulties do people in those countries where Christianity has not penetrated come to receive baptism by desire! Error is an obstacle to the Holy Ghost. This explains why the Church has always sent missionaries into all countries of the world, why thousands of them have suffered martyrdom. If salvation can be found in any religion, why cross the seas, why subject oneself to unhealthy climates, to a harsh life, to sickness and an early death? From the martyrdom of St. Stephen onwards (the first to give his life for Christ, and for this reason his feast is the day after Christmas), the Apostles set out to spread the Good News throughout the Mediterranean countries.

Would they have done this if one could be saved by worshipping Cybele or by the mysteries of Eleusis? Why did Our Lord say to them, "Go and preach the Gospel to all nations"?

It is amazing that nowadays certain people want to let everyone find his own way to God according to the beliefs prevailing in his own "cultural milieu." A bishop once told a priest who wanted to convert the little Muslims, "No, teach them to be good Muslims; that will be much better than making Catholics of them." I am assured and know for certain that before the Council the Taizé community wanted to abjure their errors and become Catholics. The authorities said to them, "No, wait. After the Council you will be the bridge between Catholics and Protestants." Those who gave this reply took on a great responsibility before God, because grace comes often only at a given moment; it may perhaps not come again. At the present time the brethren of Taizé are still outside the Church, sowing confusion in the minds of the young people who visit them.

I have spoken of the conversions which have abruptly fallen in countries like the United States—where they used to amount to 170,000 a year—and Great Britain and Holland. The missionary spirit has faded away because of the wrong definition of the Church and because of the conciliar declaration on religious liberty of which I must now speak.

XI
Religious Liberty

Among all the documents of the Council, it was the *schema* on religious liberty which led to the most acrimonious discussions. This is easily explained by the influence of the liberals and the interest taken in this matter by the hereditary enemies of the Church. Now, twenty years later, we see that our fears were not exaggerated when the text was promulgated as a declaration comprising all the concepts opposed to tradition and to the teaching of recent popes. How true it is that all false or ambiguously expressed principles will inevitably reveal their implicit errors. Later in this chapter I shall show how the attacks on Catholic education by the Socialist government in France are the logical consequence of the new definition given to religious liberty by Vatican II.

A little theology will help us toward a proper understanding of the spirit in which this declaration was drawn up. The initial—and, in fact, new—argument was based on the freedom of every man to practice inwardly and outwardly the religion of his choice, on the basis of "the dignity of the human person." In this view, liberty is based on dignity, which gives it its *raison d'être*. Man can hold any error whatever in the name of his dignity.

This is putting the cart before the horse. For whoever clings to error loses his dignity and can no longer build upon it. Rather, the foundation of liberty is truth, not dignity. "The truth will make you free," said Our Lord.

What is dignity? According to Catholic tradition, man derives dignity from his perfection, i.e. from his knowledge of the truth and his acquisition of the good. Man is worthy of respect in accordance with his intention to obey God, not in accordance with his errors, which will inevitably lead to sin. When Eve the first sinner succumbed, she said, "The serpent deceived me." Her sin and that of Adam led to the downfall of human dignity, from which we have suffered ever since.

We cannot then make the downfall the cause of liberty. On the contrary, adherence to truth and the love of God are the principles of authentic religious liberty, which we can define as the liberty to render to God the worship due to Him and to live according to His commandments.

If you have followed my argument, you see that religious liberty cannot be applied to false religions; it does not allow of being split up in this way; the only right that must be recognized by the state is that of the citizens to practice Christ's religion.

This will certainly seem an exhorbitant claim to those who do not have the Faith. But the Catholic uncontaminated by the spirit of the times will find it quite normal and legitimate. Unfortunately many Christians have lost sight of these realities: it has been so often repeated that we must respect other people's ideas, put ourselves in their place, accept their point of view. The nonsensical "everyone to his own truth" has become the rule; dialogue has become the highest cardinal virtue, dialogue which necessarily leads to concessions. Through misplaced charity the Christian has come to think that he must go one step further than his interlocutors; he is usually the only one to do so. He no longer sacrifices himself for the truth, as the martyrs did. Instead, he sacrifices the truth.

On the other hand, the increase in the number of secular states in Christian Europe has accustomed people to secularism and has led them to adapt to things contrary to the Church's teaching. But doctrine cannot be adapted; it is fixed and defined once and for all.

At the Central Preparatory Commission before the Council, two *schemas* were submitted, one by Cardinal Bea

under the title "Religious Liberty," the other by Cardinal
Ottaviani under the title, "Religious Tolerance." The first
filled fourteen pages without any reference to documents of
the Magisterium. The second covered seven pages of text
and sixteen pages of references, from Pius VI (1790) to John
XXIII (1959).

Cardinal Bea's *schema* contained, in my view and in that
of a considerable number of the Fathers, propositions not in
accord with the eternal truths of the Church. We read, for
example, "This is why we must praise the fact that in our
day liberty and religious equality are proclaimed by many
nations and by the International Organization for the Rights
of Man."

Cardinal Ottaviani, on the other hand, set forth the
question correctly: "Just as the civil power considers it right
to protect citizens from the seductions of error, so it may
also regulate and moderate the public expression of other
forms of worship and defend its citizens against the diffu-
sion of false doctrines which, in the judgment of the
Church, endanger their eternal salvation."

Leo XIII, in *Rerum Novarum*, said that the common temporal good, the aim of civil society, is not purely of the material order but is "principally a moral good." Man is organized in society for the good of all. How can one exclude the
supreme good, *i.e.*, the blessedness of heaven, from the
scheme of things?

There is another aspect of the Church's role in denying
freedom to false religions. The propagation of false ideas
naturally exerts more influence upon the weakest, the least
educated. Who will challenge the duty of the State to protect the weak? This is its primary duty, the *raison d'être* of
an organized society. It defends its subjects from outside
enemies, it protects their everyday life against thieves, mur-
derers, criminals and aggressors of all sorts. Even secular
states offer protection in the area of morals by banning, for
example, pornographic magazines (although the situation in
this respect has greatly deteriorated in France in the last
few years and is at its worst in countries like Denmark.)

Nevertheless, civilized Christian countries long retained a sense of their obligations towards the most vulnerable, particularly children. People have remained sensitive in this matter and through family associations call on the state to take the necessary measures. Radio programmes in which vice is too prominent can be banned—although nobody is obliged to listen to them—on the ground that, since many children have radios, they are no longer protected. The teaching of the Church in this regard, which might seem excessively severe, is thus in accord with reason and common sense.

It is the current fashion to reject all forms of constraint and to bemoan its influence at certain periods of history. Pope John Paul II, deferring to this fad, deplored the Inquisition during his visit to Spain. But it is only the excesses of the Inquisition that are remembered. What is forgotten is that the Church, in creating the Holy Office (*Sanctum Officium Inquisitionis*), was fulfilling its duty in protecting souls and proceeded against those who were trying to falsify the Faith and thus endangering the eternal salvation of everyone. The Inquisition came to the help of the heretics themselves, just as one goes to the help of persons who jump into the water to end their lives. Would we accuse the rescuers of exerting an intolerable constraint upon these unfortunates? To make another comparison, I do not think it would occur to a Catholic, even a confused one, to complain of a government's ban on drugs, contending that it is exercising constraint upon drug addicts.

Everyone understands that the father of a family will bring up his children in his faith. In the Acts of the Apostles the centurion Cornelius, touched by grace, received baptism "and all his household with him." King Clovis in the same way was baptized together with his soldiers.

The benefits that the Catholic religion brings with it show how deluded is the attitude of the post-conciliar clergy who renounce any pressure, or even influence, on non-believers. In Africa, where I spent the major part of my life, the missions fought against the scourges of polygamy, homosexuality, and the contempt in which women are held. The degraded position of women in Islamic society is well known: she becomes a slave or chattel as soon as Christian civilization disappears. There can be no doubt of the right of the truth to prevail and to replace false religions. And yet in practice the Church does not prescribe blindly and intransigently regarding the expression of false religions in public. She has always said that they could be tolerated by the authorities in order to avoid a great evil. That is why Cardinal Ottaviani preferred the term "religious tolerance."

If we put ourselves in the position of a Catholic state where the religion of Christ is officially recognized, we see that this tolerance can avoid troubles which may be harmful to the whole. But in a secular society professing neutrality, the law of the Church will surely not be observed. What, you will then ask, is the good of maintaining it?

First of all, it is a question of a human law that can be abrogated or altered. Secondly, abandoning a principle has serious consequences. We have already noted a number of them.

The agreements between the Vatican and certain nations which had rightly granted a privileged status to the Catholic religion have been modified. This is the situation in Spain and more recently in Italy, where the catechism is no longer compulsory in the schools. How far will they go? Have these new legislators of human nature realized that the Pope is also the head of a state? Will he be compelled to secularize the Vatican and authorize the construction of a mosque and a Protestant church in it?

Catholic states themselves are disappearing. In the world today there are Protestant States, an Anglican state, Moslem states, Marxist states—and yet they think there should be no more Catholic states! Catholics will no longer be entitled to work to establish them; they will be allowed only to maintain the religious neutrality of the state!

Pius IX called this "madness" and "the freedom of perdition." Leo XIII condemned religious indifference of the state. Is what was right in their times no longer so?

We cannot insist upon the freedom of all religious societies, within human society, without at the same time granting them moral liberty. Islam allows polygamy; Protestants—depending on the particular sect—have more of less lax positions on the indissolubility of marriage and on contraception. The criterion of good and evil is disappearing. Abortion is no longer illegal in Europe, except in Catholic Ireland. It is impossible for the Church of God to condone these abuses by affirming religious liberty.

Another consequence affects Catholic schools. The state can no longer grant that Catholic schools should exist and that they should have the lion's share of private education. It places them on the same footing, as we have seen, with the schools of non-Catholic sects, and says, "If we allow you to exist, we must do the same for the Moonies and every community of this type, even those of bad repute." And the Church cannot argue! The Socialist government in France has taken advantage of the Declaration on Religious Liberty and tried to merge Catholic schools with the others and demand that the resulting institutions observe just the natural law. Or else they have been opened to children of all religions, congratulating themselves at having more Moslem children than Christians in some areas.

This is why the Church, by accepting the status of common right in civil society, runs the risk of becoming merely one sect among others. She even runs the risk of disappearing, since it is obvious that truth cannot concede rights to error without denying itself.

The Catholic schools in France have adopted—for the purpose of public demonstrations—a certain song, which is beautiful in itself, but with words betraying the pernicious spirit of "liberty, the only truth." Liberty, considered as an absolute good, is a chimera. Applied to religion, it leads to doctrinal relativism and practical indifference. Confused Catholics must hold to the words of Christ which I quoted, "The truth will make you free."

XII
Comrades and Fellow-Travellers

Let us take up where we left off. Christian common
sense is offended in every way by this new religion. Catholics are exposed to desacralization on all sides; everything
has been changed. They are told that all religions bring salvation; the Church welcomes without distinction separated
Christians and in fact all believers, whether they bow to
Buddha or to Krishna. They are told that clergy and laity
are equal members of the "People of God," so that lay people designated for particular functions take over the
clergy's tasks. We see them conducting funerals and taking
Viaticum to the sick, while the clergy take up the functions
of the laity—dress like them, work in factories, join trade
unions and engage in politics. The new Canon Law supports all this. It confers unheard-of prerogatives on the laity, blurring the distinction between them and priests and
creating so-called "rights." Lay theologians hold chairs of
theology in Catholic universities, the faithful take over roles in
divine worship which were once reserved to those in clerical
orders: they administer some of the sacraments, they distribute Holy Communion and serve as witnesses at weddings.

We also read that the Church of God "subsists" in the
Catholic Church—a suspicious formula, because immemorial doctrine has always said that the Church of God *is* the
Catholic Church. If we accept this recent formula, it would
seem that Protestant and Orthodox communions form equal
parts of the Church—which cannot be, since they have
separated themselves from the one Church founded by Jesus Christ: *Credo in UNAM sanctam Ecclesiam.*

The new Canon Law was drawn up in such haste and confusion that, although promulgated in January 1983, a hundred and fourteen modifications had been added by November of the same year. This too is disconcerting to Christians who are accustomed to think of Church law as something permanent.

If the father of a family (whether or not a regular church-goer) wants his children to be well educated, he is bound to be disappointed. Catholic schools are in many cases mixed, sex education is given, religious instruction has disappeared in the higher classes, and it is not unusual to find teachers with Liberal or even Communist leanings. In one case which caused an uproar in the west of France, a teacher was removed owing to pressure from parents, then reinstated by diocesan authorities. He defended himself by saying, "Six months after starting at Our Lady's (School), the father of one pupil wanted to get rid of me simply because I had shown myself from the start to be left-wing in every respect—political, social and religious. According to him, one could not be both a philosophy teacher in a Catholic school and a Socialist."

Another incident occurred in the north of France. A new head teacher was appointed to a school by the diocesan authorities. After a short time the parents learned that he was a militant member of a left-wing union, that he was a laicized priest, married and with children apparently not baptized. At Christmas he organized a party for the pupils and their parents with the support of a group which was known to be Communist. In such circumstances Catholics of goodwill must wonder if it is worthwhile to make sacrifices to send their children to Catholic schools.

At a girls' school in the heart of Paris, a chaplain from the prison at Fresnes came to the catechism class, accompanied by a young (eighteen-year-old) inmate. He explained to the pupils how lonely the prisoners were, how they needed affection, outside contacts and letters. Any girl wishing to become such a "godmother" could give her name and address. But no mention of this must be made to parents because they would not understand. It had to remain confidential among the young people.

Elsewhere there was a teacher about whom complaints were received—this time from a group of parents because she had taught her children sections of the catechism and the Hail Mary. She was supported by the Bishop, as was quite right. But it seemed so unusual that his letter was reprinted in a teachers' magazine as something sensational.

What is to be made of all this? Catholic schools, when the French government decided to do away with them, proved vulnerable because in almost all cases, they had in one way or another ceased to fulfill their mission. Their opponents found it easy to say, "What are you doing for the educational system? We are doing exactly the same thing as you. Why have two systems?" Of course we still find some reservoirs of faith, and we must pay tribute to the many teachers who are conscious of their responsibilities. But Catholic education no longer asserts itself clearly when confronted with state schooling. It has gone a good halfway along the road that the zealots of secularism want it to go. I have been told that at demonstrations some groups have caused scandal by shouting, "We want God in our schools!" The organizers had secularized the songs, slogans and speeches as much as possible in order (so they said) not to embarrass those who had come along without religious positions, including unbelievers and even atheistic Socialists.

Is it dabbling in politics to want to remove Socialism and Communism from our schools? Catholics have always rightly thought that the Church was opposed to these doctrines because of the militant atheism they profess. Communism holds radically different views about the meaning of life, the destiny of nations and the way in which society is moving. It is all the more astonishing, therefore, to read in *Le Monde* for the 5th June 1984 that Mgr.Lustiger (Archbishop of Paris), in reply to questions put by the paper and while making some very correct observations along the way, complained of having seen an historical opportunity lost with Parliament's vote on Catholic schools. This opportunity, he said, consisted in finding some basic values in common with the Socialist-Communists for the education of children. What basic values can there be in common between the Marxist left and Christian doctrine? They are completely opposed to each other.

Yet Catholics observe with amazement that dialogue between the Church hierarchy and Communists is intensifying. Soviet leaders and also a terrorist such as Yasser Arafat are received at the Vatican. The Council set the fashion by refusing to renew the condemnation of Communism. Finding no mention of it in the schemas submitted to them, 450 bishops—we would do well to remember—signed a letter calling for an amendment to this effect. They were referring to previous condemnations and in particular to the statement of Pius XI which described Communism as "intrinsically evil," meaning that there are no negative and positive elements in this ideology, but that it must be rejected in its entirety. We remember what happened: the amendment was not conveyed to the Fathers. The Secretariat General said they knew nothing about it. Then the Commission admitted having received it, but too late. This is not true. It caused a scandal which ended, on the Pope's orders, with an appendix to the Constitution *Gaudium et Spes* containing an additional remark on Communism.

How many statements by bishops have been made to justify and even to encourage collaboration with Communism, regardless of what Communism professes! "It is not up to me; it is for Christians who are responsible adults," said Bishop Matagrin, "to see under what conditions they can collaborate with the Communists." For Bishop Delorme, Christians must "fight for more justice in the world alongside all those who strive for justice and freedom, including the Communists." The same tune from Bishop Poupard, who urges "working with all men of goodwill for justice in all areas where a new world is being tirelessly built up." According to one diocesan magazine, the funeral oration of a worker-priest went like this: "He opted for a world of workers on the occasion of the local council elections. He could not be everybody's priest. He chose those who made the choice of Socialist society. It was hard for him. He made enemies but also many new friends. Little Paul was a man in his place." A short while ago one bishop persuaded priests not to talk in their parishes about "Help to the Church in Need," saying, "My impression is that this work appears in too exclusively an anti-Communist light."

We notice with bewilderment that the excuse for this sort of collaboration lies in the intrinsically false idea that the aim of the Communist party is to establish justice and freedom. We must remember the words of Pius IX on this point: "If the faithful allow themselves to be deceived by those fomenting the present intrigues, if they agree to conspire with them for the evil systems of Socialism and Communism, let them realize and reflect, they are laying up for themselves treasures of vengeance on the day of wrath; and in the meantime there will come forth from this conspiracy no temporal advantage for the people but rather an increase of misery and calamities."

To see the accuracy of this warning—given in 1849, nearly 140 years ago—we need only to look at what is happening in all the countries that have come under the yoke of Communism. Events have proved the Pope of the Syllabus right, yet in spite of this the illusion remains just as bright and strong as ever. Even in Poland, a profoundly Catholic country, the pastors no longer treat the Catholic Faith and the salvation of souls as primary importance, for which all sacrifices must be accepted, including that of life itself. What matters most to them is avoiding a break with Moscow, and this enables Moscow to reduce the Polish people to an even more complete slavery without serious resistance.

Father Floridi[4] shows clearly the results of the compromise policy of the Vatican's Ostpolitik: "It is a known fact

---

4. Rev, A. U. Floridi, *Moscow and the Vatican*, Editions France Empire.

(he says) that the Czechoslovakian bishops consecrated by Cardinal Casaroli are collaborators of the regime, as are the bishops dependent on the Patriarchate of Moscow. Happy to have been able to place a bishop in each diocese of Hungary, Pope Paul VI paid homage to Janos Kadar, First Secretary of the Hungarian Communist Party and "principal promoter and authority in the normalization of relations between the Holy See and Hungary." But the Pope did not tell the high price paid for this normalization: the installation in important positions in the Church of "peace priests." In fact, Catholics were stupefied when they heard Cardinal Laszlo Lekai, the successor of Cardinal Mindszenty, promise to step up talks between Catholics and Marxists. Speaking of the intrinsic evil of Communism, Pius XI added, "and one can identify no grounds for collaboration with it by anyone who wishes to save Christian civilization."

This departure from the teaching of the Church, added to those I have already enumerated, obliges us to say that the Vatican is now occupied by Modernists and men of this world who believe there is more effectiveness to be found in human and diplomatic artifices for the salvation of the world than in what was instituted by the divine Founder of the Church.

I have mentioned Cardinal Mindszenty; like him, all the heroes and martyrs of Communism, in particular Cardinals Beran, Stepinac, Wynszinski and Slipyj, are embarrassing to present Vatican diplomats, and it must be said, are silent reproofs to them; they are now fallen asleep in the Lord.

The same contacts have been established with Freemasonry, in spite of the unambiguous declaration by the Congregation for the Faith in February 1981, which was preceded by a declaration from the German Bishops' Conference in April 1980. But the new Canon Law makes no mention of it and deliberately imposes no sanctions. Catholics have recently found that B'nai B'rith Masons have been received at the Vatican and recently the Archbishop of Paris met for talks with the Grand Master of a Masonic lodge. In the meantime, certain churchmen are trying to reconcile this

Synagogue of Satan with the Church of Christ.

They reassure Catholics by telling them, as for everything else, "The former condemnation of the sects was perhaps justified, but the Masonic brotherhood is not what it used to be." But see how they go about their work. The scandal of the P2 Lodge in Italy is still fresh in people's minds. In France there is no doubt whatever that the civil laws against Catholic private education were above all the work of Grand Orient Freemasonry, which has increased its pressure upon the President of the Republic and his associates within the government and cabinet ministries, to the end that "the great unified National education service" may at last become a reality. For once they have acted openly. Some newspapers such as *Le Monde* have given a regular account of their maneuvers; their planning and their strategy have been published in their magazines.

Do I need to point out that Freemasonry is what it has always been? The former Grand Master of the Grand Orient, Jacques Mitterand, admitted on the radio in 1969, "We have always had bishops and priests in our lodges," and made the following profession of faith: "If to place man upon the altar in place of God is the sin of Lucifer, then all humanists since the Renaissance have committed this sin." This was one of the complaints against the Freemasons when they were excommunicated for the first time by Pope Clement XII in 1738. In 1982, the Grand Master Georges Marcou said, "It is the problem of man which is paramount." At the forefront of his concerns when he was re-elected was subsidising abortion by the National Health Service, saying, "Women's economic equality depends on this step."

Freemasons have penetrated into the Church. In 1976 it was discovered that the man at the centre of the liturgical reform, Mgr. Bugnini, was a Freemason. And we can be sure he was not the only one. The veil covering the greatest mystery hidden from the clergy and faithful has begun to tear. We see more and more clearly with the passing of time—but so do the Church's secular enemies. "Something has changed within the Church," wrote Jacques Mitterand; "and replies given by the Pope to the most urgent questions, such as priestly celibacy and birth control, are hotly debated within the Church itself; the word of the Sovereign Pontiff is questioned by bishops, by priests, by the faithful. For a Freemason, a man who questions dogma is already a Freemason without an apron."

Another brother, Mr. Marsaudon of the Scottish Rite, spoke as follows of the ecumenism nurtured during the Council: "Catholics, especially the conservatives, must not forget that all roads lead to God. And they will have to accept that this courageous idea of freethinking, which we can really call a revolution, pouring forth from our Masonic lodges, has spread magnificently over the dome of St. Peter's."

I should again like to quote for you a text which throws light on this question and shows which side hopes to prevail over the other in the contacts advocated by Fr. Six and Fr. Riquet. It is an extract from the Masonic review *Humanism*, the issue for November/December 1968:

"Amongst the pillars which will collapse most easily, we mention the doctrinal power endowed with infallibility, which the First Vatican Council, one hundred years ago, believed it had strengthened and which had sustained some combined attacks following the publication of the encyclical *Humane Vitae*. The Real Presence in the Eucharist, which the Church succeeded in imposing on the medieval masses, will disappear with progress in intercommunion and concelebration between Catholic priests and Protestant pastors: the sacred character of the priest, which derives from the institution of the sacrament of orders, will give place to an elective and temporary role; the distinction between the hierarchy and the lower clergy will yield to the dynamic working from the base upwards, just as in every democracy; and there will be the gradual disappearance of the ontological and metaphysical nature of the sacraments and most certainly the end of confession, sin having become in our civilization one of the most anachronistic notions that we have inherited from the harsh philosophy of the Middle Ages, which itself was heir to biblical pessimism."

You notice how interested the Freemasons are in the Church's future—in order to devour her. Catholics need to be aware of this, in spite of the sirens who would sing them to sleep. All those destructive forces are closely interrelated. Freemasonry describes itself as the philosophy of Liberalism, which in its most extreme form is Socialism. The whole comes under the phrase used by our Lord: "the gates of hell."

XIII
Religious Liberty, Collegial Equality, Ecumenical Fraternity

How does it happen that the gates of hell are now causing us so much trouble? The Church has always been disturbed by persecution and heresies, by conflicts with temporal powers, sometimes by immoral conduct of the clergy, sometimes even of popes. But this time the crisis seems to go much deeper, since it affects the Faith itself. The Modernism we face is not a heresy like the others: it is the main drain of all heresies. Persecution now comes not only from outside but from within the Church. The scandal of dissolute living, or just giving up, has become endemic among the clergy, while the mercenaries who abandon the sheep to the wolves are encouraged and honored. I am sometimes accused of painting too black a picture of the situation, of viewing it too disapprovingly, of taking pleasure at being disgruntled over changes which are perfectly logical and necessary. Yet the same Pope who was the heart and soul of Vatican II commented several times on the decomposition on which I have commented so sadly. On 7th December 1969 Paul VI said, "The Church finds herself in a period of anxiety, of self-criticism, one could say of self-destruction. It is like an internal upheaval, serious and complex—as if the Church were flagellating herself."

The following year he added, "In many areas the Council has not so far given us peace but rather stirred up troubles and problems that in no way serve to strengthen the Kingdom of God within the Church or within souls." Then, going on to raise a cry of alarm, on 29th June 1972 (Feast of St. Peter and St. Paul), "The smoke of Satan has entered by some crack into the temple of God; doubt, uncertainty, problems, restlessness, dissatisfaction and confrontation have come to the surface... doubt has entered our consciences."

Where is the crack? We can pinpoint the time with precision. It was 1789, and its name, the Revolution. The Masonic and anti-Catholic principles of the French Revolution have taken two hundred years to enter tonsured and mitred heads. Today this is an accomplished fact. Such is the reality and the cause of your perplexities, my confused Catholic readers. The facts had to be before our eyes for us to believe them, because we thought a priori that an undertaking of this sort was impossible and incompatible with the very nature of the Church, assisted as it is by the Spirit of God.

In a well known article written in 1877, Bishop Gaume gave us a personification of the Revolution. "I am not what you think I am. Many speak of me but few know me. I am not Freemasonry, nor rioting, nor the changing of the monarchy into a republic, not the substitution of one dynasty for another, not temporary disturbance of public order. I am not the shouts of Jacobins, nor the fury of the Montagne, nor the fighting on the barricades, nor pillage, nor arson, nor the agricultural law, nor the guillotine, nor the drownings. I am neither Marat nor Robespierre, nor Babeuf nor Mazzini nor Kossuth. These men are my sons but they are not me. These things are my works but they are not me. These men and these things are passing objects but I am a permanent state... I am the hatred of all order not established by man and in which he himself is not both king and god."

Here is the key to the "changes" in the Church; replacing a divine institution with one set up by man, in which man takes precedence over God. Man ruling over everything, everything having its beginning and its ending in him; to him we bow down.

Paul VI described this turnabout in his speech at the

end of the Council: "Profane and secular humanism has shown itself in its own terrible stature and has in a sense defied the Council. The religion of God made Man has come up against the religion of man who makes himself God." He immediately added that in spite of this terrible challenge, there has been no clash, no anathema. Alas! By making a display of a "boundless sympathy for all men", the Council failed in its duty to point out clearly that no compromise is possible between the two attitudes. Even the closing speech seemed to give an impetus to what we are seeing put into daily practice. "You can be grateful to it (the Council) for this merit at least, you modern humanists who deny the transcendence of the supreme things, and learn to recognize our new humanism: we too, we more than anyone else, subscribe to the cult of man."

Afterwards we heard coming from the same lips statements developing this theme. "Men are basically good and incline towards reason, towards order and the common good" (Peace Day Message, 14th November 1970). "Both Christianity and democracy have a basic principle in common; respect for the dignity and for the value of the human person... the advancement of the complete man" (Manila, 20th November 1970). How can we not be dismayed by this comparison when democracy, which is a specifically secular system, ignores in man his characteristic as a redeemed child of God, the only quality which grants him dignity? The advancement of man is certainly not the same thing when seen by a Christian and by an unbeliever.

The pontifical message becomes more secularized on each occasion. At Sydney on 3rd December 1970, we were startled to hear, "Isolation is no longer permissible; the time has come for a great solidarity amongst mankind and the establishment of a worldwide united and brotherly community." Peace amongst all men, certainly, but Catholics are no longer acknowledging the words of Christ, "My peace I give to you, not as the world gives, give I unto you." The bond which unites earth to heaven seems to be broken. "Ah well, we live in a democracy! That means the people are in charge; power comes from numbers, from the people" (Paul VI, 1st January 1970). Jesus said to Pilate, "You would have no power over me if it had not been given to you from above." Power comes from God and not from numbers, even if the choice of the leader has been made by an elective process. Pilate was the representative of a pagan nation and yet he could do nothing without the permission of the Heavenly Father.

And now we have democracy entering into the Church. The new Canon Law teaches that power resides in the "People of God." This tendency towards bringing what they call the base into sharing the exercise of power can be found all through present structures—synod, episcopal conferences, priests' councils, pastoral councils, Roman commissions, national commissions, etc.; and there are equivalents in the religious orders.

This democratization of the Magisterium represents a mortal danger for millions of bewildered and infected souls to whom the spiritual doctors bring no relief because it has ruined the efficacy with which the personal Magisterium of the Pope and bishops was formerly endowed. A question concerning faith or morals is submitted to numerous theological commissions, who never come up with an answer because their members are divided both in their opinions and in their methods. We need only read the procedural accounts of the assemblies at all levels to realize that collegiality of the Magisterium is equivalent to paralysis of the magisterium.

Our Lord instructed individuals, not a collectivity, to tend His sheep. The Apostles obeyed Our Lord's orders, and until the twentieth century it was thus. These days we hear of the Church being in a state of permanent council, continual collegiality. The results have become apparent. Everything is upside down, the faithful no longer know which way to turn.

The democratization of government was followed quite naturally by the democratization of the Magisterium which took place under the impulse of the famous slogan "collegiality," spread abroad by the communist, Protestant and progressive press.

They have collegialized the pope's government and that of the bishops with a presbyterial college, that of the parish priest with a lay council, the whole broken down into innumerable commissions, councils, sessions, etc. The new Code of Canon Law is completely permeated with this concept. The pope is described as the head of the College of Bishops. We find this doctrine already suggested in the Council document *Lumen Gentium*, according to which the College of Bishops, together with the pope, exercises supreme power in the Church in habitual and constant manner. This is not a change for the better; this doctrine of double supremacy is contrary to the teaching and Magisterium of the Church. It is contrary to the definitions of Vatican Council I and to Pope Leo XIII's encyclical *Satis Cognitum*. The Pope alone has supreme power; he communicates it only to the degree he considers advisable, and only in exceptional circumstances. The pope alone has power of jurisdiction over the whole world.

We are witnessing therefore a restriction on the freedom of the Supreme Pontiff. Yes, this is a real revolution! The facts demonstrate that what we have here is not a change without practical consequences. John Paul II is the first pope to be really affected by the reform. We can quote several precise instances where he has reconsidered a decision under pressure from a bishops' conference. The Dutch Catechism received the *imprimatur* from the Archbishop of Milan without the modifications requested by the Commission of Cardinals. It was the same with the Canadian Catechism. In that connection I heard someone in authority in Rome say, "What can we do when faced with a bishops' conference?" The independence assumed by the conferences has also been illustrated in France with regard to the catechisms. The new books are contrary in almost every respect to the *Apostolic Exhortation Catechesi Tradendae*. The *ad limina* visit by the bishops of the Paris area in 1982 consisted in their getting the Pope to ratify a catechism which he openly disapproved. The allocution delivered by John Paul II at the end of the visit had all the signs of a compromise, thanks to which the bishops were able to return in triumph to their own country and continue with their pernicious practices. Cardinal Ratzinger's lectures in Paris and Lyons indicate clearly that Rome has not endorsed the reasons given by the French bishops for installing a new doctrine and orientation, but the Holy See has been reduced by this kind of pressure to proceeding by suggestions and advice, instead of issuing the orders needed to put things on the right track, and when necessary to condemn, as the popes have hitherto always done, as guardians of the deposit of faith.

The bishops, whose authority would thereby seem to be increased, are the victims of a collegiality which paralyzes the running of their dioceses. So many complaints are made on this subject by the bishops themselves, complaints which are very instructive! In theory the bishop can in a number of cases act against the wishes of the assembly. Sometimes even against the majority, if the voting has not been submitted to the Holy See for approval; but in practice this has proved impossible. Immediately after the end of the meeting its decisions are published by the secretary. They are thus known to all priests and faithful; the news media divulge all the essentials. What bishop could in fact oppose these decisions without showing his disagreement with the assembly and then immediately finding himself confronted with a number of revolutionary spirits who would appeal against him to the assembly?

The bishop has become the prisoner of collegiality, which should have been limited to a consultative group, not a decision-making body. Even for the simplest things he is no longer master of his own house.

Soon after the Council, while I was on a visitation of our communities, the bishop of a diocese in Brazil came very obligingly to meet me at the railway station. "I can't put you up at the bishop's house," he said, "but I have had a room prepared for you at the minor seminary." He took me there himself; the place was in an uproar—young men and girls everywhere, in the corridors and on the stairs. "These young men, are they seminarians?" I asked. "Alas, no. Believe me, I am not at all happy at having these young people at my seminary, but the Bishops' Confererce has decided that we must from now on hold Catholic Action meetings in our houses. These you see are here for a week. What can I do? I can only do the same as the others."

The powers conferred upon persons by divine right, whether pope or bishops, have been confiscated for the benefit of a group whose ascendency continues to grow. Bishops' conferences, some will say, are not a recent thing. Pius X gave them his approval at the beginning of this century. That is correct, but that holy pope gave them a definition which justified them. "We are persuaded that these bishops' assemblies are of the greatest importance for the maintenance and development of God's kingdom in all regions and all provinces. Whenever the bishops, the guardians of holy things, thereby bring their lights together, the result is that not only do they better perceive their people's needs and choose the most suitable remedies, but they thereby also tighten the bonds uniting them."

Consequently, they were bodies that did not make decisions binding on their members in an authoritarian manner, any more than do congresses of scientists decide the way in which experiments must be carried out in this or that laboratory.

The bishops' conference, however, now works like a parliament; the permanent council of the French episcopate is its executive body. The bishop is more like a prefect or a commissioner of the Republic (to use the fashionable terminology) than a successor of the Apostles charged by the pope to govern a diocese.

In these assemblies they vote; the ballots are so numerous that at Lourdes they have had to install an electronic voting system. This results inevitably in the creation of parties. The two things do not happen one without the other. Parties mean divisions. When the regular government is subjected to the consultative vote in its normal functioning, then it is rendered ineffective. Consequently the whole body suffers.

The introduction of collegiality has led to a considerable weakening in efficacy, in that the Holy Ghost is more easily impeded and saddened by an assembly than by an individual. When persons are responsible, they act, they speak, even if some say nothing. At meetings, it is the majority who decide. Yet numbers do not make for the truth. Nor do they make for efficiency, as we have learnt after twenty years of collegiality and as we might have presupposed without making the experiment. The fable-writer spoke long ago of the "many chapters which have been held for nothing." Was it necessary to copy the political systems in which decisions are justified by voting (since they no longer have sovereign heads)? The Church possesses the immense advantage of knowing what she must do to further the Kingdom of God. Her leaders are appointed. So much time is wasted in elaborate joint statements, which are never satisfactory, because they have to take everyone's opinion into account! So much travelling to take part in commissions and sub-commissions, in select committees and preparatory meetings! Bishop Etchgaray said at Lourdes at the close of the 1978 Assembly, "We no longer know which way to turn."

The result is that the Church's powers of resistance to Communism, heresy, immorality, have been considerably weakened. This is what its opponents have been hoping for and that is why they made such efforts, at the time of the Council and after it, to urge her into the ways of democracy.

If we look carefully, it is by means of its slogan that the Revolution has penetrated the Church. "Liberty"—this is the religious liberty we spoke of earlier, which confers rights on error. "Equality"—collegiality and the destruction of personal authority, the authority of God, of the pope, of the bishops; in a word, majority rule. Finally, "Fraternity" is represented by ecumenism.

By these three words, the revolutionary ideology of

1789 has become the Law and the Prophets. The Modernists have achieved what they wanted.

XIV
"Vatican II is the French Revolution in the Church"

The parallel I have drawn between the crisis in the Church and the French Revolution is not simply a metaphorical one. The influence of the *philosophes* of the eighteenth century, and of the upheaval that they produced in the world, has continued down to our times. Those who have injected that poison into the Church admit it themselves. It was Cardinal Suenens who exclaimed, "Vatican II is the French Revolution in the Church," and among other unguarded declarations he added, "One cannot understand the French or the Russian revolutions unless one knows something of the old regimes which they brought to an end... It is the same in Church affairs: a reaction can only be judged in relation to the state of things that preceded it." What preceded, and what he considered due for abolition, was that wonderful hierarchical construction culminating in the Pope, the Vicar of Christ on earth. He continued: "The Second Vatican Council marked the end of an epoch; and if we stand back from it a little more we see it marked the end of a series of epoches, the end of an age."

Pere Congar, one of the artisans of the reforms, spoke likewise: "The Church has had, peacefully, its October Revolution." Fully aware of what he was saying, he remarked "The Declaration on Religious Liberty states the opposite of the Syllabus." I could quote numbers of admissions of this sort. In 1976 Fr. Gelineau, one of the party-leaders at the National Pastoral and Liturgical Center removed all illusions from those who would like to see in the

Novus Ordo something merely a little different from the rite which hitherto had been universally celebrated, but in no way fundamentally different: "The reform decided on by the Second Vatican Council was the signal for the thaw... Entire structures have come crashing down. Make no mistake about it. To translate is not to say the same thing with other words. It is to change the form. If the form changes, the rite changes. If one element is changed, the totality is altered... it must be said, without mincing words, the Roman rite we used to know exists no more. It has been destroyed."[5]

The Catholic liberals have undoubtedly established a revolutionary situation. Here is what we read in the book written by one of them, Monsignor Prelot,[6] a senator for the Doubs region of France. "We had struggled for a century and a half to bring our opinions to prevail within the Church and had not succeeded. Finally, there came Vatican II and we triumphed. From then on the propositions and principles of liberal Catholicism have been definitively and officially accepted by Holy Church."

It is through the influence of this liberal Catholicism that the Revolution has been introduced under the guise of pacifism and universal brotherhood. The errors and false principles of modern man have penetrated the Church and contaminated the clergy thanks to liberal popes themselves, and under cover of Vatican II.

It is time to come to the facts. To begin with, I can say that in 1962 I was not opposed to the holding of a General Council. On the contrary, I welcomed it with great hopes. As present proof here is a letter I sent out in 1963 to the Holy Ghost Fathers and which has been published in one of my previous books.[7] I wrote: "We may say without hesitation, that certain liturgical reforms have been needed, and it

---

5. *Demain la liturgie*, ed. du Cerf.
6. *Le Catholicisme Liberal*, 1969
7. *A Bishop Speaks*, The Angelus Press.

is to be hoped that the Council will continue in this direction." I recognized that a renewal was indispensable to bring an end to a certain sclerosis due to a gap which had developed between prayer, confined to places of worship, and the world of action—schools, the professions and public life. I was nominated a member of the Central Preparatory Commission by the Pope and I took an assiduous and enthusiastic part in its two years of work. The central commission had the responsibility of checking and examining all the preparatory schemas which came from the specialist commissions. I was in a good position therefore to know what had been done, what was to be examined, and what was to be brought before the assembly.

This work was carried out very conscientiously and meticulously. I still possess the seventy-two preparatory schemas; in them the Church's doctrine is absolutely orthodox. They were adapted in a certain manner to our times, but with great moderation and discretion.

Everything was ready for the date announced and on 11th October, 1962, the Fathers took their places in the nave of St. Peter's Basilica in Rome. But then an occurrence took place which had not been foreseen by the Holy See. From the very first days, the Council was besieged by the progressive forces. We experienced it, felt it; and when I say we, I mean the majority of the Council Fathers at that moment.

We had the impression that something abnormal was happening and this impression was rapidly confirmed; fifteen days after the opening session not one of the seventy-two schemas remained. All had been sent back, rejected, thrown into the waste-paper basket. This happened in the following way. It had been laid down in the Council rules that two-thirds of the votes would be needed to reject a preparatory schema. Now when it was put to the vote there were 60% against the schemas and 40% in favor. Consequently the opposition had not obtained the two-thirds, and normally the Council would have proceeded on the basis of the preparations made.

It was then that a powerful, a very powerful organization showed its hand, set up by the Cardinals from those countries bordering the Rhine, complete with a well-organized secretariat. They went to find the Pope, John XXIII, and said to him: "This is inadmissible, Most Holy Father; they want us to consider schemas which do not have the majority," and their plea was accepted. The immense work that had been accomplished was scrapped and the assembly found itself empty-handed, with nothing ready. What chairman of a board meeting, however small the company, would agree to carry on without an agenda and without documents? Yet that is how the Council commenced.

Then there was the affair of the Council commissions which had to be appointed. This was a difficult problem; think of the bishops arriving from all countries of the world and suddenly finding themselves together in St. Peter's. For the most part, they did not know one another; they knew three or four colleagues and a few others by reputation out of the 2400 who were there. How could they know which of the Fathers were the most suitable to be members of the commission for the priesthood, for example, or for the liturgy, or for canon law?

Quite lawfully, Cardinal Ottaviani distributed to each of them the list of the members of the pre-conciliar commissions, people who in consequence had been selected by the Holy See and had already worked on the subjects to be debated. That could help them to choose without there being any obligation and it was certainly to be hoped that some of these experienced men would appear in the commissions.

But then an outcry was raised. I don't need to give the name of the Prince of the Church who stood up and made the following speech: "Intolerable pressure is being exerted upon the Council by giving names. The Council Fathers must be given their liberty. Once again the Roman Curia is seeking to impose its own members."

This crude outspokenness was rather a shock, and the session was adjourned. That afternoon the secretary, Mgr. Felici, announced "The Holy Father recognizes that it would perhaps be better for the bishops' conferences to meet and draw up the lists."

The bishops' conferences at that time were still embryonic: they prepared as best they could the lists they had been asked for without, anyway, having been able to meet as they ought, because they had only been given twenty-four hours. But those who have woven this plot had theirs all ready with individuals specially chosen from various countries. They were able to forestall the conferences and in actual fact they obtained a large majority. The result was that the commissions were packed with two-thirds of the members belonging to the progressivist faction and the other third nominated by the Pope.

New schemas were rapidly brought out, of a tendency markedly different from the earlier ones. I should one day like to publish them both so that one can make the comparison and see what was the Church's doctrine on the eve of the Council.

Anyone who has experience of either civil or clerical meetings will understand the situation in which the Fathers found themselves. In these new schemas, although one could modify a few odd phrases or a few propositions by means of amendments, one could not change their essentials. The consequences would be serious. A text which is biased to begin with can never be entirely corrected. It retains the imprint of whoever drafted it and the thoughts that inspired it. The Council from then on was slanted. A third element contributed to steering it in a liberal direction. In place of the ten presidents of the Council who had been nominated by John XXIII, Pope Paul VI appointed for the last two sessions four moderators, of whom the least one can say is that they were not chosen among the most moderate of the cardinals. Their influence was decisive—for the majority of the Council Fathers.

The liberals constituted a minority, but an active and organized minority, supported by a galaxy of modernist theologians amongst whom we find all the names who since then have laid down the law, names like Leclerc, Murphy,

Congar, Rahner, Kung, Schillebeeckx, Besret, Cardonnel, Chenu, etc. And we must remember the enormous output of printed matter by IDOC, the Dutch Information Center, subsidized by the German and Dutch Bishops' Conferences which all the time was urging the Fathers to act in the manner expected of them by international opinion. It created a sort of psychosis, a feeling that one must not disappoint the expectations of the world which is hoping to see the Church come round to its views. So the instigators of this movement found it easy to demand the immediate adaptation of the Church to modern man, that is to say, to the man who wants to free himself of all restraint. They made the most of a Church deemed to be sclerotic, out of date, and powerless, beating their breasts for the faults of their predecessors. Catholics were shown to be more guilty than the Protestants and Orthodox for their divisions of times past; they should beg pardon of their "separated brethren" present in Rome, where they had been invited in large numbers to take part in the activities.

The Traditional Church having been culpable in its wealth and in its triumphalism, the Council Fathers felt guilty themselves at not being in the world and at not being of the world; they were already beginning to feel ashamed of their episcopal insignia; soon they would be ashamed to appear wearing the cassock.

This atmosphere of liberation would soon spread to all areas. The spirit of collegiality was to be the mantle of Noah covering up the shame of wielding personal authority, so contrary to the mind of twentieth century man, shall we say, liberated man! Religious freedom, ecumenism, theological research, and the revising of canon law would attenuate the triumphalism of a Church which declared itself to be the sole Ark of Salvation. As one speaks of people being ashamed of their poverty, so now we have ashamed bishops, who could be influenced by giving them a bad conscience. It is a technique that has been employed in all revolutions. The consequences are visible in many places in the annals of the Council. Read again the beginning of the schema, "The Church in the Modern World," on the changes in the world today, the accelerated movement of history, the new conditions affecting religious life, and the predominance of science and technology. Who can fail to see in these passages an expression of the purest liberalism?

We would have had a splendid council by taking Pope Pius XII for our master on the subject . I do not think there is any problem of the modern world and of current affairs that he did not resolve, with all his knowledge, his theology and his holiness. He gave almost definitive solutions, having truly seen things in the light of faith.

But things could not be seen so when they refused to make it a dogmatic council. Vatican II was a pastoral Council; John XXIII said so, Paul VI repeated it. During the course of the sittings we several times wanted to define a concept; but we were told: "We are not here to define dogma and philosophy; we are here for pastoral purposes." What is liberty? What is human dignity? What is collegiality? We are reduced to analyzing the statements indefinitely in order to know what they mean, and we only come up with approximations because the terms are ambiguous. And this was not through negligence or by chance. Fr. Schillebeeckx admitted it: "We have used ambiguous terms during the Council and we know how we shall interpret them afterwards." Those people knew what they were doing. All the other Councils that have been held during the course of the centuries were dogmatic. All have combatted errors. Now God knows what errors there are to be combatted in our times! A dogmatic council would have filled a great need. I remember Cardinal Wyszinsky telling us: "You must prepare a schema upon Communism; if there is a grave error menacing the world today it is indeed that. If Pius XII believed there was need of an encyclical on communism, it would also be very useful for us, meeting here in plenary assembly, to devote a schema to this question."

Communism, the most monstrous error ever to emerge from the mind of Satan, has official access to the Vatican. Its world-wide revolution is particularly helped by the official non-resistance of the Church and also by the frequent support it finds there, in spite of the desperate warnings of those cardinals who have suffered in several of the Eastern countries. The refusal of this pastoral council to condemn it solemnly is enough in itself to cover it with shame before the whole of history, when one thinks of the tens of millions of martyrs, of the Christians and dissidents scientifically de-personalized in psychiatric hospitals and used as human guinea-pigs in experiments. Yet the Council kept quiet. We obtained the signatures of 450 bishops calling for a declaration against Communism. They were left forgotten in a drawer. When the spokesman for *Gaudium et Spes* replied to our questioning, he told us "There have been two petitions calling for a condemnation of Communism." "Two!" we cried, "there are more than 400 of them!" "Really, I know nothing about them." On making inquiries, they were found, but it was too late.

These events I was involved in. It is I who carried the signatures to Mgr. Felici, the Council Secretary, accompanied by Mgr. de Proenca Sigaud, Archbishop of Diamantina: and I am obliged to say there occurred things that are truly inadmissible. I do not say this in order to condemn the Council; and I am not unaware that there is here a cause of confusion for a great many Catholics. After all, they think the Council was inspired by the Holy Ghost.

Not necessarily. A non-dogmatic, pastoral council is not a recipe for infallibility. When, at the end of the sessions, we asked Cardinal Felici "Can you not give us what the theologians call the 'theological note of the Council'?" He replied, "We have to distinguish according to the schemas and the chapters those which have already been the subject of dogmatic definitions in the past; as for the declarations which have a novel character, we have to make reservations."

Vatican II therefore is not a Council like others and that is why we have the right to judge it, with prudence and reserve. I accept in this Council and in the reforms all that is in full concordance with Tradition. The Society I have

founded is ample proof. Our seminaries in particular com-
ply with the wishes expressed by the Council and with the
ratio fundamentalis of the Sacred Congregation for Catholic
Education.

But it is impossible to maintain it is only the later appli-
cations of the Council that are at fault. The rebellion of the
clergy, the defiance of pontifical authority, all the excesses
in the liturgy and the new theology, and the desertion of
the churches, have they nothing to do with the Council, as
some have recently asserted? Let us be honest: they are its
fruits!

In saying this I realize that I merely increase the worry
and perplexity of my readers. But, however, among all this
tumult a light has shone forth capable of reducing to
nought the attempts of the world to bring Christ's Church
to an end. On the 30th June 1968 the Holy Father published
his Profession of Faith. It is an act which from the dogmatic
point of view is more important than all the Council.

This Credo, drawn up by the successor of Peter to affirm the faith of Peter, was an event of quite exceptional
solemnity. When the Pope rose to pronounce it the Cardinals rose also and all the crowd wished to do likewise, but
he made them sit down again. He wanted to be alone, as
Vicar of Christ, to proclaim his Credo and he did it with the
most solemn of words, in the name of the Blessed Trinity,
before the holy angels and before all the Church. In consequence, he has made an act which pledges the faith of the
Church.

We have thereby the consolation and the confidence of
feeling that the Holy Ghost has not abandoned us. We can
say that the Act of Faith that sprang from the First Vatican
Council has found its other resting point in the profession
of faith of Paul VI.

XV
The Marriage of the Church
and the Revolution

The Revolution, it has been said, expresses "the hatred
of all order that has not been established by man, and in
which he is not both king and god." At its origin we find
that pride which had already been the cause of Adam's sin.
The revolution within the Church can be explained by the
pride of men of our times who believe they are in a new
age when man has finally "understood his own dignity,"
and has acquired an increased awareness of himself "to the
extent that one might speak of a social and cultural meta-
morphosis whose efforts have had repercussions on religious life. The very pace of history is becoming so rapid that
one is hard pressed to keep up with it. In short, the human
race is passing from a mainly static conception of the order
of things to a dynamic and evolutive conception. The consequence is an immense series of new problems which call for
new analyses and new syntheses." These wonder-struck
phrases which, with many others of the same sort, occur in
the Introduction to *Gaudium et Spes*, the Pastoral Constitution on the Church in the Modern World, are of ill-omen for
a return to the spirit of the Gospel. In so much change and
transformation, it is hard to see how this can survive.

And what is meant by the statement: "An industrial
type of society is spreading little by little, radically trans-
forming our ideas about life in society" except that the
writer is prophesying as a certainty what he wanted to see
appear: a concept of society that will have nothing in common with the Christian concept expressed in the social doc-

trine of Church? Presuppositions of that nature can lead
only to a new Gospel and a new religion. And here it is!
"The faithful, therefore, ought to work in close conjunction
with their contemporaries to try to get to know their ways
of thinking and feeling as they find them expressed in current cultures. Let the faithful incorporate the findings of
new sciences and teachings and the understanding of the
most recent discoveries with Christian morality and
thought, so that their practice of religion and moral behavior may keep abreast of their acquaintance with science and
of the relentless progress of technology: in this way they
will evaluate and interpret everything with an authentically
Christian sense of values."[8] Strange advice, considering that
we are commanded by the Gospel to shun perverse doctrines! And let it not be said that these theories can be understood in two ways: the current catechisms understand
them in the way Schillebeeckx wanted. They advise children to listen to what atheists have to say because they
have much to learn from them; and besides, if they do not
believe in God they have their reasons, and these are worth
knowing! And the opening phrase of the first chapter, "Believers and unbelievers agree almost unanimously that all
things on earth should be ordained to man as to their center
and summit" can also be said to be given a Christian meaning by what follows. It has, nevertheless, a meaning in itself
which is exactly what we see being put into effect everywhere in the post-conciliar Church, in the shape of a salvation reduced to economic and social well-being.

For my part, I think that those who accept this proposition as a common basis for dialogue with unbelievers, and
couple new theories with Christian doctrine, will lose their
faith, neither more nor less. The golden rule of the Church
has been inverted by the pride of the men of our time. No

---

8. *Gaudium et Spes*, 62. Translation from *Vatican Council II*, ed. by A. Flan-
nery, O.P., Fowler Wright Books (1975).

one listens any more to Christ's ever-living and fruitful words, but to those of the world. This "aggiornamento" condemns itself. The roots of present-day disorder are to be found in this modern, or rather modernist spirit which refuses to recognize the creed, the commandments of God and the Church, the sacraments, and Christian morality as the only source of renewal until the end of the world. Dazzled by "technical progress which will eventually go on to transform the face of the earth and already is embarking on the conquest of space" (*Gaudium et Spes* 5-1) churchmen, who must not be confused with the Church, appear to think that Our Lord could not have foreseen the present-day technological evolution and that consequently his message is no longer appropriate.

The liberal's dream for the last century and a half has been to unite the Church to the revolution. For a century and a half also, the Popes have condemned liberal catholicism. Among their most important documents we can mention the bull *Auctorem fidei* by Pius VI against the Council of Pistoia, the encyclical *Quanta cura* and the *Syllabus* of Pius IX, the encyclical *Immortale Dei* of Leo XIII against the new Right, the acts of St. Pius X against the *Sillon* and modernism, especially the decree *Lamentabili*, the encyclical *Divini Redemptoris* of Pius XI against Communism and the encyclical *Humani Generis* of Pope Pius XII.

All these Popes have resisted the union of the Church with the revolution; it is an adulterous union and from such a union only bastards can come. The rite of the new mass is a bastard rite, the sacraments are bastard sacraments. We no longer know if they are sacraments which give grace or do not give it. The priests coming out of the seminaries are bastard priests, who do not know what they are. They are unaware that they are made to go up to the altar, to offer the sacrifice of Our Lord Jesus Christ and to give Jesus Christ to souls.

In the name of the revolution, priests have been sent to the scaffold, nuns have been persecuted and murdered. Remember the pontoons of Nantes which were sunk out at sea after they had filled them with faithful priests. And yet what the revolution did is nothing compared to the doings of Vatican II, because it would have been better for those twenty or thirty thousand priests who have abandoned their priesthood and the vows made before God, to have been martyred and sent to the scaffold. They would at least have saved their souls, whereas now they risk losing them.

It is said that amongst these poor married priests many have already been divorced, many have already applied to Rome for nullity of marriage. Can this be called the good fruit of the Council? And twenty thousand nuns in the United States and very many in other countries, have broken the perpetual vows which united them to Jesus Christ to run off and get married. If they had mounted the scaffold they would at least have born witness to their faith. The blood of the martyrs is the seed of Christians, but the priests or simple faithful who surrender to the spirit of the world will not bring forth a harvest. The devil's greatest victory is to have undertaken the destruction of the Church without making any martyrs.

The adulterous union of the Church and the Revolution is cemented by "dialogue." Our Lord said "Go, teach all nations and convert them." He did not say "Hold dialogue with them but don't try to convert them." Truth and error are incompatible; to dialogue with error is to put God and the devil on the same footing. This is what the Popes have always repeated and what was easy for Christians to understand because it is also a matter of common sense. In order to impose different attitudes and reactions it was necessary to do some indoctrinating so as to make modernists of the clergy needed to spread the new doctrine. This is what is called "recycling," a conditioning process intended to refashion the very faculty God gave man to direct his judgment.

I have witnessed an operation of this sort in my own congregation of which I was for a time the Superior General. The *first* thing required is to "accept change." The Council has introduced changes, therefore we also must change. Change in depth, since it is a case of adapting the reasoning faculties to make them coincide with arbitrarily conceived notions. We can read in a booklet issued by the Archbishop's Office in Paris "The Faith Word by Word": "The *second* operation is more delicate and consists of registering the different ways that Christians have of reacting, in these various changes, to the very fact of change. This registering is important because actual opposition is due more to a spontaneous and sub-conscious attitude in the face of change, than to precise issues involved in the change.

"Two typical attitudes can be discerned, while allowing for the possibility of intermediate ones. The first means accepting a number of novelties one by one as they are imposed. This is the case with many Christians, many Catholics: they give in little by little.

"Those who take the second attitude accept a total renewal of the expression of the Christian faith at the threshold of a new cultural era, while always taking care to keep close to the faith of the Apostles."

This last phrase is a typical rhetorical safeguard of the modernists. They always protest that their attitudes are orthodox, and seek to reassure by little phrases those who would be alarmed at such prospects as "the total renewal of the expression of Christian faith on the threshold of a new cultural era." But one is already far gone when one accepts such reassurances; and much good it will do to venerate the faith of the Apostles when one has demolished the faith entirely.

A *third* operation becomes necessary when this second attitude is encountered: "The inquirer cannot help feeling now that his faith is dangerously at risk. Will it not simply vanish, together with the problems that have brought it to that point? He therefore requires some fundamental assurance which will enable him to go beyond these sterile initial reasonings."

So all degrees of resistance have been foreseen. What is the "fundamental assurance" that will be given the neophyte in the last resort? The Holy Ghost! "It is precisely the

Holy Ghost who assists believers in the turning points of history ."

The goal is achieved: there is no longer any Magisterium, no dogma, nor hierarchy; not Holy Scripture even, in the sense of an inspired and historically certain text. Christians are inspired directly by the Holy Ghost.

The Church then collapses. The recycled Christian becomes subject to every influence and receptive to every slogan; he can be led anywhere, while grasping, if he needs reassurance, at the declaration: "Vatican II assuredly shows many signs of a change in the terms of the inquiry."

"The direct and immediate cause (of Modernism) lies in a perversion of the mind," wrote St. Pius X in his encyclical *Pascendi*. Recycling creates a similar mental perversion in those who did not previously suffer from it. The holy Pope also quoted this observation of his predecessor Gregory XVI: "It is a sorry sight to see how far the deviations of human reason will go as soon as one yields to the spirit of novelty; when, heedless of the Apostle's warning, one claims to know more than one needs to know, and self-confidently seeks for truth outside the Church instead of within it, where it is to be found without the least shadow of error."[9]

---

9. *Singulari Nos,* 1834.

XVI
Neo-Modernism or the Undermining of the Faith

In the complete revision which has taken place in the Church's vocabulary, a few words have survived, and Faith is one of them. The trouble is that it is used with so many different meanings. There is, however, a definition of faith, and that cannot be changed. It is to this that a Catholic must refer when he no longer understands anything of the garbled and pretentious language addressed to him.

Faith is "the adherence of the intellect to the truth revealed by the Word of God." We believe in a truth that comes from outside and which is not in some way produced by our own mind. We believe it because of the authority of God who reveals it to us, and there is no need to seek elsewhere.

No one has the right to take this faith from us and replace it by something else. What we are now seeing is the revival of a Modernist definition of faith which was condemned eighty years ago by Pius X. According to this, faith is an internal feeling: there is no need to seek further than man to find the explanation of religion: "It is therefore within man himself that it is to be found; and since religion is one form of life, it is found in the very life of man" — something purely subjective, an adhering of the soul to God, Who is inaccessible to our intellect. It is everyone for himself, in his own conscience.

Modernism is not a recent invention, nor was it in 1907, the year of the famous encyclical. It is the perennial spirit of the Revolution, and it seeks to shut us up within our human-ness and make God an outlaw. Its false definition of faith is directed to the destruction of the authority of God and the authority of the Church.

Faith comes to us from outside, and we have an obligation to submit to it. "He who believes will be saved, and he who does not believe will be condemned;" Our Lord Himself affirms it.

When I went to see the Pope in 1976, to my very great surprise he reproached me for making my seminarists swear an oath against him. I found it hard to conceive where that idea had come from. It had evidently been whispered to him with the intention of harming me. Then it dawned on me that someone had maliciously interpreted in this way the Anti-Modernist Oath which until recently every priest had to take before his ordination, and every Church dignitary when he received his office. His Holiness Paul VI had sworn it more than once. Now here is what we find in this oath: "I hold most certainly and I profess sincerely that Faith is not a blind religious feeling which emerges from the shadows of the subsconscious under the pressure of the heart and the inclination of the morally informed will. But it is true assent of the intellect to the truth received from outside, by which we believe to be true on God's authority all that has been said, attested and revealed by God in person, our Creator and Lord."

This Anti-Modernist Oath is no longer required before becoming a priest or a bishop. If it were, there would be even fewer ordinations than there are. In effect, the concept of faith has been falsified and many people without any wrong intention let themselves be influenced by modernism. That is why they are ready to believe that all religions save. If each man's faith is according to his conscience—if it is conscience that produces faith—then there is no reason to believe that one faith saves any better than another, so long as the conscience is directed towards God. We read statements of this sort in a document from the French Bishops' Catechetical Commission: "Truth is not something received, ready-made, but something which develops."

The two view-points are completely different. We are now being told that man does not receive truth but constructs it. Yet we know, and our intelligence corroborates this, that truth is not created—we do not create it.

Then how can we defend ourselves against these perverse doctrines that are ruining religion, all the more since the "purveyors of novelties" are found in the very bosom of the Church? Thank God, they were unmasked at the beginning of the century in a way that allows them to be easily recognized. And we must not think of it as an old phenomenon of interest only to Church historians. *Pascendi* is a text that could have been written today; it is extraordinarily topical and depicts the "enemies within" with admirable vividness.

We see them "lacking in serious philosophy and theology and passing themselves off, all modesty forgotten, as restorers of the Church . . . contemptuous of all authority, chafing at every restriction." "Their tactics are never to expound their doctrines methodically and as a whole, but in some manner to split them up and scatter them about here and there. This makes them seem hesitant and imprecise, when on the contrary, their ideas are perfectly fixed and consistent. One page of their writings could have been written by a Catholic; turn over, and you will think you are reading something by a Rationalist. Reprimanded and condemned, they go their own way, concealing a boundless effrontery under a deceitful appearance of submission. Should anyone be so mistaken to criticize any one of their novelties, however outrageous, they will fall upon him in serried ranks: the one who denies it is treated as an ignoramus, while whoever accepts and defends it is praised to the skies. A publication appears breathing novelty at every pore: applause and cries of admiration greet it. The more audacious a writer is in belittling antiquity and in undermining Tradition and the Church's magisterium, the cleverer he is. Finally, should one of them incur the Church's condemnation, the others will immediately rally round him, eulogise him publicly and venerate him almost as a martyr for the truth."

All these features correspond so closely with what we are seeing that we could imagine them to have been written just recently. In 1980, after the condemnation of Hans Küng, a group of Christians took part in an *auto-da-fè* in front of the Cologne cathedral as a form of protest against the Holy See's decision to withdraw from the Swiss theologian his canonical mandate. A bonfire was made, and on it they threw an effigy and writings of Küng "in order to symbolize the repression of courageous and honest thought" (*Le Monde*). Shortly before that, the sanctions against Père Pohier had provoked another public outcry. Three hundred Dominican friars and nuns signed another text; the abbey of Bouquen, the Chapel of Montparnasse, and other avant-garde groups leapt into the fray. The only new thing, by comparison with Pius X's description, is that they no longer hide under the cover of submission. They have gained confidence; they have too much support within the Church to conceal themselves any longer. Modernism is not dead; on the contrary, it progresses and flaunts itself.

To continue with *Pascendi*: "After that, we need not be surprised that the modernists pursue those Catholics who fight energetically for the Church, with all their malice and harshness. There is no limit to the insults they will heap on them. If the adversary is one redoubtable on account of his learning and intellect they will try to make him powerless by organizing around him a conspiracy of silence." This is what is happening today to hounded and persecuted traditionalist priests, and to clerical and lay religious writers concerning whom the press, in the hands of the progressivists, never says a word. Youth movements too are shunned for the fact that they remain faithful, and their edifying activities, pilgrimages and so forth remain unknown to the public who might have been much encouraged by them.

"If they write history, they seek out with curiosity everything that seems to them to be a blot on the Church's history; and they expose it to the public with ill-dissimulated pleasure under the pretence of telling the whole truth. Dominated as they are by their preconceptions, they destroy as far as they are able the pious traditions of the people. Certain relics that are most venerable on account of their antiquity they hold up to ridicule. Lastly, they are obsessed by the vanity of wanting to have themselves talked about, which, as they well know, would not happen if they spoke as people have always spoken hitherto."

As for their doctrine, it is based on the following few points which we have no difficulty in recognizing in current thought. "Human reason is incapable of raising itself up to God, or even of knowing, from the fact of created beings, that He exists." As any external revelation is impossible, man will seek within himself to satisfy the need he feels for the divine, a need rooted in his subsconscious. This need arouses in the soul a particular feeling "which in some way unites man with God." This is what faith is for the modernists. God is thereby created within the soul, and that is Revelation.

From the sphere of religious feeling we pass to that of the intellect, which proceeds to elaborate the basic dogmas: since man is endowed with intelligence, he has a need to think out his faith. He creates formulas, which do not contain absolute truth but only images or symbols of the truth. Consequently these dogmatic formulas are subject to change, they evolve. "Thereby the way is open for substantial changes in dogmas."

The formulas are not simply theological speculations, they have to be living to be truly religious. Man's feeling for religion, religious sentiment, needs to assimilate them "vitally." "Living the faith" is a current phrase. Continuing in St. Pius X's exposition of Modernism, we read, "These formulas, if they are to be living formulas, must always be suited to the believer and to his faith. The day they cease to be so, they will automatically lose their original content, and then there will be nothing to do but change them. Since dogmatic formulas, as the Modernists conceive them, are of such an unstable and precarious nature, one understands

perfectly why they have such a slight opinion of them, even
if they do not despise them openly. Religious *feeling*, religious *life* are the phrases always on their lips." And in their
sermons, lectures and catechisms, "ready-made formulas"
are anathema.

The believer makes his personal experience of faith,
then he communicates it verbally to others, and in that way
religious experience propagates itself. Once the faith has become common or, as one says, collective, the need is felt to
combine together in a society to preserve and develop the
common treasure. This is how a Church is formed. The
Church is "the fruit of the collective conscience, in other
words, of the sum of individual consciences, which all de-
rive from one original believer—who for Catholics is Jesus
Christ."

And this is how the modernists write the history of the
Church: at the beginning, when the Church's authority was
still believed to come from God, it was conceived as an
autocratic body. "But now the mistake has been realized.
For just as the Church is a vital emanation of the collective
conscience, so Authority in its turn is a vital product of the
Church." Power, therefore, must change hands and come
from the bottom. As political consciousness has created
popular government, the same thing must happen in the
Church: "If ecclesiastical authority does not wish to pro-
voke a crisis of conscience, it must bow to democratic
forms."

You will now understand where Cardinal Suenens and
all the talkative theologians got their ideas. The post-conciliar crisis is in complete continuity with the crisis which
disturbed the end of the last century and the beginning of
this one. You will also understand why, in the catechism
books that your children bring home with them, everything
begins with the first communities that were formed after
Pentecost, when the disciples, as a consequence of the shak-
ing-up which the meeting with Jesus provoked in them, felt
a need of the divine and lived out a "new experience" together. And you can now explain the absence of dogmas—

such as the Holy Trinity, the Incarnation, the Redemption and the Assumption—in these books and also in sermons. The *Texte de référence* or teacher's handbook for the catechism prepared by the French episcopate covers also the creating of groups which will be "mini-churches" destined to re-create tomorrow's Church on the lines that the modernists thought they could discern at the birth of the Apostolic Church: "In the catechism group, teachers, parents and children contribute their experiences of life, their deep yearnings, religious imagery and a certain knowledge of the things of faith. A confrontation ensues which is a condition of truth to the extent that it stirs up their deep aspirations and produces an authentic commitment to the changes that any contact with the Gospel inevitably produces. It is only after the experience of a separation, a conversion, a sort of death, that by the help of grace a confession of faith can be made."

So it is the bishops who put into effect, in broad daylight, the modernist tactics condemned by St. Pius X! It is all in this paragraph[10]—read it again carefully: religious feeling stirred up by a need, deep yearnings, truth that takes shape in the sharing of experiences, the changing of dogmas and the breach with Tradition. For the modernists the sacraments, too, originate in a need, "for as has been observed, in their system necessity or need is the great all-embracing explanation." Religion needs a tangible body: "The sacraments (for them) are simply signs of symbols, although endowed with efficacy. They compare them to certain words which have a vogue because of their power of expressing and disseminating impressive, inspiring ideas. As much as to say that the sacraments were only instituted to nourish faith: a proposition which the Council of Trent condemned."

One finds this idea again, to take an example, in the

---

10. *Texte de reference*, para. 312.

writings of Besret, who was an "expert" at the Council: "It
is not the sacrament which brings God's love into the
world. His love is at work in every man. The sacrament is
the moment of its public manifesting in the community of
the disciples . . . In saying this, I in no way intend to deny
the efficacious aspect of the sacramental signs. Man fulfils
himself by self-expression, and that is true for the sacraments as it is for the rest of his activity."[11]

And the books of Holy Writ? For the Modernists, they
are "the record of experiences undergone in a given religion." God speaks through these books, but He is the God
who is within us. The books are inspired rather as one
speaks of poetic inspiration; inspiration is likened to the urgent need felt by the believer to communicate his faith in
writing. The Bible is human work.

In *Pierres Vivantes,*[12] the children are told that Genesis is
"a poem" written once upon a time by believers who "had
reflected." This compilation, imposed on all catechism children by the French episcopate, exudes Modernism on
nearly every page. Let us draw up a short parallel:

ST. PIUS X: "It is a law (for the modernists) that the
dates of the documents cannot be determined otherwise
than by the dates of the needs which successively made
themselves felt in the Church"

PIERRES VIVANTES: "To help these communities to
live the Gospel, some of the Apostles wrote them letters,
also called Epistles...but above all the Apostles related by
word of mouth what Jesus had done among them and what
He had said. Later on, four writers—Mark, Matthew, Luke
and John—put into writing what the Apostles had said."
Dates of the Gospels: Mark about 70 A.D.? Luke about 80-
90? Matthew about 80-90? John about 95-100. They re-
counted the events of Jesus's life, His words and especially

11. *Decommencement en commencement,* p. 165.
12. See Chapter VIII.

His death and resurrection *to enlighten the faith of the believers.*"

ST. PIUS X: "In the sacred scriptures (they say) there are many places where science or history enter, where obvious errors are to be found. Yet it is not history or science that these books are treating of, but solely religion and morality."

PIERRES VIVANTES: "The book (Genesis) is a poem, not a science manual. Science tells us that it took millions of years for life to appear." "The Gospels do not tell the story of the life of Jesus in the same way that today events are reported on the radio or the television or in the newspaprs."

ST. PIUS X: "They do not hesitate to affirm that the books in question, expecially the Pentateuch and the first three Gospels, were gradually formed by additions made to a very short original narrative: interpolations in the form of theological or allegorical interpretations, or simply linking-passages and tackings-on."

PIERRES VIVANTES: "What is written in most of these books had previously been related orally from father ot son. One day someone wrote it down to transmit it in his turn; and often what he wrote was re-written by others for yet other people... 538, the Persian domination: reflections and traditions become books. About 400 B.C. Esdras collects together various books to make of them the Law or Pentateuch. The scrolls of the Prophets are composed. The reflections of the Sages produce various masterpieces."

Catholics who wonder at the new language employed in the "Conciliar Church" will be helped by knowing that it is not so new: that Lammenais, Fuchs and Loisy were already using it in the last century, and that they themselves had only picked up all the errors which had been current for ages. But the religion of Christ has not changed and never will: we must not let ourselves be imposed upon.

XVII
What is Tradition?

Modernism is indeed what undermines the Church from within, today as yesterday. Let us again quote from the encyclical *Pascendi* some typical features which correspond with what we are experiencing now. "The Modernists say that Authority in the Church, since its end is purely spiritual, should strip itself of all that external pomp, all those pretentious adornments with which it parades itself in public. In this they forget that religion, while it belongs to the soul, is not exclusively for the soul and that the honor paid to authority is reflected back on Christ who institutes it."

It is under pressure from these "speakers of novelties" that Paul VI abandoned the tiara, bishops gave up the violet cassock and even the black, as well as their rings, and priests appear in lay clothes, usually in a deliberately casual style. There is nothing among the general reforms already put into effect or insistently demanded that St. Pius X has not mentioned as the "maniac" desires of the modernist reformers. You will recognize them in this passage: "As regards worship (they want) to diminish the number of external devotions or at least stop their increasing . . . Let ecclesiastical government become democratic; let a share in the government be given to the junior clergy and even the laity; let authority be decentralized. Reform of the Roman Congregations, above all the Holy Office and the Index . . . Finally there are those among them who, echoing their Protestant masters, seek the suppression of priestly celibacy."

Notice that the same demands are now being put forward and that there is absolutely nothing original. As regards Christian thought and the formation of future priests, the intention of the reformers of St. Pius X's time was the abandonment of scholastic philosophy among the obsolete systems." They advocate "that young people should be taught modern philosophy, the only true philosophy, the only one suitable for our times... that so-called rational theology should be based on modern philosophy and positive theology on the history of dogmas." In this respect, the Modernists have got what they wanted and more. In what passes for seminaries, they teach anthropology, psychoanalysis and Marx in place of St. Thomas Aquinas. The principles of Thomist philosophy are rejected in favor of vague systems which themselves recognize their inability to explain the economy of the Universe, putting forward as they do the philosophy of the absurd. One latter-day revolutionary, a muddle-headed priest much heeded by intellectuals, who put sex at the heart of everything, was bold enough to declare at public meetings: "The scientific hypotheses of the ancients were pure nonsense and it is on such nonsense that St. Thomas and Origen based their systems." Immediately afterwards, he fell into the absurdity of defining life as "an evolutionary chain of biologically inexplicable facts." How can he know that, if it is inexplicable? How, I would add, can a priest discard the only explanation, which is God?

The Modernists would be set at naught if they had to defend their elaborate theories against the principles of the Angelic Doctor, the notions of potency and act, essence, substance and accidents, body and soul, etc. By eliminating these notions they would render the theology of the Church incomprehensible and, as one reads in the Motu Proprio *Doctoris Angelici,* "the result is that students of the sacred disciplines no longer even perceive the meaning of the words by which the dogmas which God has revealed are propounded by the Magisterium." The offensive against scholastic philosophy is a necessary preliminary when one wants to change dogma and attack Tradition.

But what is Tradition? It seems to me that the word is often imperfectly understood. It is equated to the "traditions" that exist in trades, in families and in civic life: the "bouquet" fixed to the roof of a house when the last tile is laid, the ribbon that is cut to open a monument, etc. That is not what I am referring to: Tradition does not consist of the customs inherited from the past and preserved out of loyalty to the past even where there are no clear reasons for them. Tradition is defined as *the Deposit of Faith transmitted by the Magisterium down through the centuries*. This deposit is what has been given to us by Revelation; that is to say, the Word of God entrusted to the Apostles and transmitted unfailingly by their successors.

But now they want to get everyone inquiring, searching, as if we had not been given the Creed, or as if Our Lord had not come to bring us the Truth once and for all. What do they claim to discover with all this inquiry? Catholics upon whom they would impose these "questionings," after having made them "abandon their certainties," should remember this: the deposit of Revelation concluded at the death of the last Apostle. It is finished and it cannot be touched until the end of time. Revelation is irreformable. The First Vatican Council re-stated this explicitly: "for the doctrine of faith which God has revealed has not been proposed, like a philosophical invention, to be perfected by human ingenuity; but has been delivered as a divine deposit to the Spouse of Christ (the Church) to be faithfully kept and infallibly declared."

But, one will object, the dogma that makes Mary the Mother of God only dates back to the year 431, transubstantiation to 1215, papal infallibility to 1870 and so on. Has there not been an evolution? No, not at all. The dogmas which have been defined in the course of the ages were contained in Revelation; the Church has just made them explicit. When Pope Pius XII defined in 1950 the dogma of the Assumption, he said specifically that this truth of the assumption into Heaven of the Virgin Mary, body and soul, was included in the deposit of Revelation and already existed in the texts revealed to us before the death of the last Apostle. We cannot bring anything new into this field, we cannot add a single dogma, but only express those that exist ever more clearly, more beautifully and more loftily.

That is so certain that it forms the rule to follow in judging the errors that are put before us every day, and rejecting them with no concession. As Bossuet forcefully wrote: "When it is a matter of explaining the principles of Christian morality and the essential dogmas of the Church everything that does not appear in the Tradition of all time, and especially the early times, is from then on not only suspect but wrong and to be condemned; and this is the principal basis on which all the holy Fathers of the Church, and Popes more than anyone, condemned false doctrines, there being nothing more odious to the Roman Church than novelties."

The argument that is pressed upon the terrorized faithful is this: "You are clinging to the past, you are being nostalgic; live in your own time!" Some are abashed and do not know what to reply. Nevertheless, the answer is easy: In this there is no past or present or future. Truth belongs to all times, it is eternal.

In order to break down Tradition they confront it with Holy Scripture, after the manner of the Protestants, with the assertion that the Gospel is the only book that counts. But Tradition came before the Gospel! Although the Synoptic Gospels were not written nearly as late as some would have us believe, a number of years had passed before the Four Evangelists had completed their writing; but the Church already existed, Pentecost had taken place and brought numerous conversions, 3000 on the very day the Apostles came out of the Upper Room. What did they believe just at that moment? How was Revelation transmitted if not by oral tradition? One cannot subordinate Tradition to Holy Scripture, still less reject it.

But do not imagine that, adopting this attitude, they have an unlimited respect for the inspired text. They even dispute that it is inspired in its entirety: "What is there in the Gospel which is inspired? Only the truths that are necessary for our salvation." In consequence, the miracles, the accounts of the Holy Childhood, the actions and conduct of Our Lord are relegated to the category of more or less legendary biography. We fought in the Council over that phrase: "Only the truths necessary for salvation." There were some bishops in favor of reducing the historical authenticity of the Gospels, which shows the extent to which the clergy is corrupted by neo-Modernism. Catholics should not allow themselves to be imposed upon: the whole of the Gospel is inspired and those who wrote it had the Holy Ghost guiding their intelligence, so that the whole of it is the Word of God, *Verbum Dei*. It is not permissible to pick and choose and to say today: "We will take this part but we don't want that part." To choose is to be a heretic, according to the Greek derivation of that word.

It remains no less a fact that it is Tradition that transmits the Gospel to us, and it appertains to Tradition, to the Magisterium, to explain to us the contents of the Gospel. If we have nobody to interpret it for us, we can reach several completely different understandings of the same words of Christ. We then end up with the free interpretation of the Protestants and the free inspiration of the present day charismatics which leads us into pure fantasy.

All the dogmatic councils have given us the exact expression of Tradition, the exact expression of what the Apostles taught. Tradition is irreformable. One can never change the decrees of the Council of Trent, because they are infallible, written and published by an official act of the Church, unlike those of Vatican II, which pronouncements are not infallible because the popes did not wish to commit their infallibility. Therefore nobody can say to you, "You are clinging to the past, you have stayed with the Council of Trent." For the Council of Trent is not the past. Tradition is clothed with a timeless character, adapted to all times and all places.

XVIII
True and False Obedience

Indiscipline is everywhere in the Church. Committees of priests send demands to their bishops, bishops disregard pontifical exhortations, even the recommendations and decisions of the Council are not respected and yet one never hears uttered the word "disobedience," except as applied to Catholics who wish to remain faithful to Tradition and just simply keep the Faith.

Obedience is a serious matter; to remain united to the Church's Magisterium and particularly to the Supreme Pontiff is one of the conditions of salvation. We are deeply aware of this and nobody is more attached to the present reigning successor of Peter, or has been more attached to his predecessors, than we are. I am speaking here of myself and of the many faithful driven out of the churches, and also of the priests who are obliged to celebrate Mass in barns as in the French Revolution, and to organize alternative catechism classes in town and country.

We are attached to the Pope for as long as he echoes the apostolic traditions and the teachings of all his predecessors. It is the very definition of the successor of Peter that he is the keeper of this deposit. Pius IX teaches us in *Pastor Aeternus:* "The Holy Ghost has not in fact been promised to the successors of Peter to permit them to proclaim new doctrine according to His revelations, but to keep strictly and to expound faithfully, with His help, the revelations transmitted by the Apostles, in other words the Deposit of Faith."

The authority delegated by Our Lord to the Pope, the

Bishops and the priesthood in general is for the service of faith. To make use of law, institutions and authority to annihilate the Catholic Faith and no longer to transmit life, is to practise spiritual abortion or contraception.

This is why we are submissive and ready to accept everything that is in conformity with our Catholic Faith, as it has been taught for two thousand years, but we reject everything that is opposed to it.

For the fact is that a grave problem confronted the conscience and the faith of all Catholics during the Pontificate of Paul VI. How could a Pope, true successor of Peter, assured of the assistance of the Holy Ghost, preside over the most vast and extensive destruction of the Church in her history within so short a space of time, something that no heresiarch has ever succeeded in doing? One day this question will have to be answered.

In the first half of the Fifth Century, St. Vincent of Lérins, who was a soldier before consecrating himself to God and acknowledged having been "tossed for a long time on the sea of the world before finding shelter in the harbor of faith," spoke thus about the development of dogma: "Will there be no religious advances in Christ's Church? Yes, certainly, there will be some very important ones, of such a sort as to constitute progress in the faith and not change. What matters is that in the course of ages knowledge, understanding and wisdom grow in abundance and in depth, in each and every individual as in the churches; provided always that there is identity of dogma and continuity of thought." Vincent, who had experienced the shock of heresies, gives a rule of conduct which still holds good after fifteen hundred years: "What should the Catholic Christian therefore do if some part of the Church arrives at the point of detaching itself from the universal communion and the universal faith? What else can he do but prefer the general body which is healthy to the gangrenous and corrupted limb? And if some new contagion strives to poison, not just a small part of the Church but the whole Church at once, then again his great concern will be to attach himself to Antiquity which obviously cannot any more be seduced by any deceptive novelty."

In the Rogation-tide litanies the Church teaches us to say: "We beseech thee O Lord, maintain in Thy holy religion the Sovereign Pontiff and all the orders of ecclesiastical hierarchy." This means that such a disaster could very well happen.

In the Church there is no law or jurisdiction which can impose on a Christian a diminution of his faith. All the faithful can and should resist whatever interferes with their faith, supported by the catechism of their childhood. If they are faced with an order putting their faith in danger of corruption, there is an overriding duty to disobey.

It is because we judge that our faith is endangered by the post-conciliar reforms and tendencies, that we have the duty to disobey and keep the Tradition. Let us add this, that the greatest service we can render to the Church and to the successor of Peter is to reject the reformed and liberal Church. Jesus Christ, Son of God made man, is neither liberal nor reformable. On two occasions I have heard emissaries of the Holy See say to me: "The social Kingdom of Our Lord is no longer possible in our times and we must ultimately accept the plurality of religions." This is exactly what they have said to me.

Well, I am not of that religion. I do not accept that new religion. It is a liberal, modernist religion which has its worship, its priests, its faith, its catechism, its ecumenical Bible translated jointly by Catholics, Jews, Protestants and Anglicans, all things to all men, pleasing everybody by frequently sacrificing the interpretation of the Magisterium. We do not accept this ecumenical Bible. There is the Bible of God; it is His Word which we have not the right to mix with the words of men.

When I was a child the Church everywhere had the same faith, the same sacraments and the same Sacrifice of the Mass. If anyone had told me then that it would be changed, I would not have believed him. Throughout the breadth of Christendom we prayed to God in the same way. The new liberal and modernist religion has sown division.

Christians are divided within the same family because of this confusion which has established itself; they no longer go to the same Mass and they no longer read the same books. Priests no longer know what to do; either they obey blindly what their superiors impose on them, and lose to some degree the faith of their childhood and youth, renouncing the promises they made when they took the Anti-Modernist Oath at the moment of their ordination; or on the other hand they resist, but with the feeling of separating themselves from the Pope, who is our father and the Vicar of Christ. In both cases, what a heartbreak! Many priests have died of sorrow before their time.

How many more have been forced to abandon the parishes where for years they had practised their ministry, victims of open persecution by their hierarchy in spite of the support of the faithful whose pastor was being torn away! I have before me the moving farewell of one of them to the people of the two parishes of which he was priest: "In our interview on the....the Bishop addressed an ultimatum to me, to accept or reject the new religion; I could not evade the issue. Therefore, to remain faithful to the obligation of my priesthood, to remain faithful to the Eternal Church... I was forced and coerced against my will to retire... Simple honesty and above all my honor as a priest impose on me an obligation to be loyal, precisely in this matter of divine gravity (the Mass)... This is the proof of faithfulness and love that I must give to God and men and to you in particular, and it is on this that I shall be judged on the last day along with all those to whom was entrusted the same deposit (of faith)."

In the Diocese of Campos in Brazil, practically all the clergy have been driven out of the churches after the departure of Bishop Castro-Mayer, because they were not willing to abandon the Mass of all time which they celebrated there until recently.

Division affects the smallest manifestations of piety. In

Val-de-Marne, the diocese got the police to eject twenty-five Catholics who used to recite the Rosary in a church which had been deprived of a priest for a long period of years. In the diocese of Metz, the bishops brought in the Communist mayor to cancel the loan of a building to a group of traditionalists. In Canada six of the faithful were sentenced by a Court, which is permitted by the law of that country to deal with this kind of matter, for insisting on receiving Holy Communion on their knees. The Bishop of Antigonish had accused them of "deliberately disturbing the order and the dignity of religious service." The judge gave the "disturbers" a conditional discharge for six months! According to the Bishop, Christians are forbidden to bend the knee before God! Last year, the pilgrimage of young people to Chartres ended with a Mass in the Cathedral gardens because the Mass of St. Pius V was banned from the Cathedral itself. A fortnight later, the doors were thrown open for a spiritual concert in the course of which dances were performed by a former Carmelite nun.

Two religions confront each other; we are in a dramatic situation and it is impossible to avoid a choice, but the choice is not between obedience and disobedience. What is suggested to us, what we are expressly invited to do, what we are persecuted for not doing, is to choose an appearance of obedience. But even the Holy Father cannot ask us to abandon our faith.

We therefore choose to keep it and we cannot be mistaken in clinging to what the Church has taught for two thousand years. The crisis is profound, cleverly organized and directed, and by this token one can truly believe that the master mind is not a man but Satan himself. For it is a master-stroke of Satan to get Catholics to disobey the whole of Tradition in the name of obedience. A typical example is furnished by the "aggiornamento" of the religious societies. By obedience, monks and nuns are made to disobey the laws and constitutions of their founders, which they swore to observe when they made their profession. Obedience in this case should have been a categorical refusal. Even legitimate authority cannot command a reprehensible and evil act. Nobody can oblige anyone to change his monastic vows into simple promises, just as nobody can make us become Protestants or modernists. St. Thomas Aquinas, to whom we must always refer, goes so far in the *Summa Theologica* as to ask whether the "fraternal correction" prescribed by Our Lord can be exercised towards our superiors. After having made all the appropriate distinctions he replies: "One can exercise fraternal correction towards superiors when it is a matter of faith."

If we were more resolute on this subject, we would avoid coming to the point of gradually absorbing heresies. At the beginning of the Sixteenth Century the English underwent an experience of the kind we are living through, but with the difference that it began with a schism. In all other respects the similarities are astonishing and should give us cause to ponder. The new religion which was to take the name "Anglicanism" started with an attack on the Mass, personal confession and priestly celibacy. Henry VIII, although he had taken the enormous responsibility of separating his people from Rome, rejected the suggestions that were put to him, but a year after his death a statute authorized the use of English for the celebration of the Mass. Processions were forbidden and a new order of service was imposed, the "Communion Service" in which there was no longer an Offertory. To reassure Christians another statute forbade all sorts of changes, whereas a third allowed priests to get rid of the statues of the saints and of the Blessed Virgin in the churches. Venerable works of art were sold to traders, just as today they go to antique dealers and flea-markets.

Only a few bishops pointed out that the Communion Service infringed the dogma of the Real Presence by saying that Our Lord gives us His Body and Blood spiritually. The *Confiteor*, translated into the vernacular, was recited at the same time by the celebrant and the faithful and served as an absolution. The Mass was transformed into a meal or Communion. But even clear-headed bishops eventually accepted the new Prayer Book in order to maintain peace and unity. It is for exactly the same reasons that the post-Conciliar Church wants to impose on us the Novus Ordo. The English bishops in the Sixteenth Century affirmed that the Mass was a "memorial!" A sustained propaganda introduced Lutheran views into the minds of the faithful. Preachers had to be approved by the Government.

During the same period the Pope was only referred to as the "Bishop of Rome." He was no longer the father but the brother of the other bishops and in this instance, the brother of the King of England who had made himself head of the national church. Cranmer's Prayer Book was composed by mixing parts of the Greek liturgy with parts of Luther's liturgy. How can we not be reminded of Mgr. Bugnini drawing up the so-called Mass of Paul VI with the collaboration of six Protestant "observers" attached as experts to the *Concilium* for the reform of the liturgy? The Prayer Book begins with these words, "The Supper and Holy Communion, commonly called Mass . . .", which foreshadows the notorious Article 7 of the *Institutio Generalis* of the New Missal, revived by the Lourdes Eucharistic Congress in 1981: "The Supper of the Lord, otherwise called the Mass." The destruction of the sacred, to which I have already referred, also formed part of the Anglican reform. The words of the Canon were required to be spoken in a loud voice, as happens in the "Eucharists" of the present day.

The Prayer Book was also approved by the bishops "to preserve the internal unity of the Kingdom." Priests who continued to say the "Old Mass" incurred penalties ranging from loss of income to removal pure and simple, with life imprisonment for further offences. We have to be grateful that these days they do not put traditionalist priests in prison.

Tudor England, led by its pastors, slid into heresy without realizing it, by accepting change under the pretext of adapting to the historical circumstances of the time. Today the whole of Christendom is in danger of taking the same road. Have you thought that even if we who are of a certain age run a smaller risk, children and younger seminarists brought up in new catechisms, experimental psychology and sociology, without a trace of dogmatic or moral theology, canon law or Church history, are educated in a faith which is not the true one and take for granted the new-Protestant notions with which they are indoctrinated? What will tomorrow's religion be if we do not resist?

You will be tempted to say:"But what can we do about it? It is a bishop who says this or that. Look, this document comes from the Catechetical Commission or some other official commission."

That way there is nothing left for you but to lose your faith. But you do not have the right to react in that way. St. Paul has warned us: "Even if an angel from Heaven came to tell you anything other than what I have taught you, do not listen to him."

Such is the secret of true obedience.

XIX
The Seminary of Ecône and Rome

You are perhaps, perplexed readers, among those who observe the course of events with sadness and anguish but are nevertheless afraid to attend a true Mass, in spite of the desire to do so, because they have been persuaded that this Mass is forbidden. You may be one of those who no longer follow the priests in anoraks but who view with some distrust the priests in cassocks as if they were under some kind of censure; is not the bishop who ordained them suspended *a divinis?* You are afraid of putting yourself out of the Church; this fear is of praiseworthy origin but it is uninformed. I want to tell you what the position is about these sanctions which have been given such prominence and caused such loud rejoicing among the Freemasons and the Marxists. To understand it properly a little history is needed.

When I was sent to Gabon as a missionary, my bishop immediately appointed me as Professor at the Seminary of Libreville, where for six years I formed seminarians, of whom some later received the grace of the episcopate. When I became a bishop in my turn, at Dakar, it seemed to me that my principal concern should be to look for vocations, to form the young men who responded to the call of God and to lead them to the priesthood. I had the joy of conferring the priesthood on one destined to be my successor at Dakar, Mgr. Thiandoum, and on Mgr. Dionne, the present Archbishop of Thiés in Senegal.

Returning to Europe to take up the position of Superior General of the Holy Ghost Fathers, I tried to maintain the essential values of priestly formation. I have to admit that already by then at the beginning of the Sixties, the pressure was such and the difficulties so considerable that I could not achieve the results I wanted. I could not keep the French Seminary in Rome, which was placed under the authority of our Congregation, on the same right lines as when we were there ourselves between 1920 and 1930. I resigned in 1968 in order not to endorse the reform undertaken by the General Chapter in a direction contrary to Catholic tradition. Already before that date I was getting numerous calls from families and from priests asking me where to send young men desiring to enter the priesthood. I admit that I was very hesitant. Freed from my responsibilities, and at a time when I was thinking of retirement, my mind turned to the University of Fribourg in Switzerland, still orientated toward Thomist doctrine. The Bishop, Mgr. Charrière, received me with open arms. I rented a house and we received nine seminarians who followed the University course and the rest of the time led the life of a real seminary. They very soon showed the desire to work together in the future and, after thinking it over, I went to ask Mgr. Charrière if he would agree to sign a decree for the foundation of a "Fraternity." He approved its statutes and thus was born on the 1st November 1970 the "Priestly Fraternity of St. Pius X." We were canonically instituted in the Diocese of Fribourg.

These details are important as you will see. A bishop has the right, canonically, to establish in his diocese associations which Rome recognizes *ipso facto*. It follows from this that if a succeeding bishop wishes to suppress an association or fraternity, he cannot do so without recourse to Rome. The authority of Rome protects what the first bishop has created so that associations are not subjected to an insecurity harmful to their development. This is how it is willed by the Law of the Church.[13]

The Priestly Society of St. Pius X is consequently recognized

13. Canon 493.

by Rome in a perfectly legal manner, although this is by
diocesan and not by pontifical decree, the latter not being
absolutely necessary. There exist hundreds of religious congregations founded on diocesan decrees which have houses
throughout the world.

When the Church recognizes a foundation or diocesan
association, she accepts that it will train its own members; if
it is a religious congregation she accepts that there will be a
noviciate or house of formation. For us, this means our
seminaries. On the 18th February 1971, Cardinal Wright,
Prefect of the Sacred Congregation for the Clergy, sent me a
letter of encouragement in which he expressed confidence
that the Fraternity "would be well able to fit in with the
objective sought by the Council in this holy Dicastery with
a view to supplying clergy for the world." However, in November 1972 at the Plenary Assembly of the French bishops
at Lourdes, it was called a "rebel seminary" without protest
from any bishops present, although they must certainly
have known the juridical situation of the Ecône seminary.

Why did they consider us rebels? Because we did not
give the key of the house to seminarians to go out in the
evenings when they felt like it, because we did not let them
watch television from 8.00 p.m. to 11.00 p.m., because they
did not wear polo-necks and went to Mass every morning
instead of staying in bed until the first lecture.

On the other hand Cardinal Garrone,[14] whom I met at
that time, said to me: "You are not directly answerable to
me and I have only one thing to say to you; follow the *ratio
fundamentalis* that I have laid down for the foundation of
seminaries, which all seminaries must follow." The *ratio fundamentalis* provides that Latin should still be taught in a
seminary and that the studies should be pursued according
to the doctrine of St. Thomas. I allowed myself to reply:
"Your Eminence, I believe we are one of the few who do

---

14. Prefect of the Congregation for Catholic Education.

follow it." This is even more true today and the *ratio fundamentalis* is still in force. So what are they reproaching us with?

When it became necessary to open a real seminary and I had rented the house at Ecône, a former rest house of the Great St. Bernard monks, I went to see Mgr. Adam, Bishop of Sion, who gave me his consent. This establishment was not the result of a long thought-out plan that I had made, it thrust itself upon me providentially. I had said: "If the work expands world-wide, that will be the sign that God is with it." From year to year the number of seminarians increased; in 1970 there were eleven entrants and in 1974, forty. The innovators became increasingly worried. It was obvious that if we were training seminarians it was to ordain them, and that the future priests would be faithful to the Mass of the Church, the Mass of Tradition, the Mass of all time. There is no need to look any further for reasons for the attacks on us; one would not find any others. Ecône appeared as a danger for the Neo-modernist church and it was important to guard against it before it was too late.

So it was on the 11th November 1974 there arrived at the seminary with the first snows two Apostolic Visitors sent by a commission appointed by Paul VI and consisting of three Cardinals, Garrone, Wright and Tabera, this last being Prefect of the Sacred Congregation for Religious. They (the Apostolic Visitors) questioned ten professors and twenty of the 104 students present, as well as myself, and departed two days later leaving a disagreeable impression behind them. They had made some scandalous remarks to the seminarians, considering the ordination of married men to be normal, declaring that they did not acknowledge an immutable Truth and expressed doubts about the traditional conception of Our Lord's Resurrection. Of the seminary they said nothing and they left no formal statement. After which, angry at the remarks they had made, I published a declaration which began with these phrases:

"We adhere with all our heart and all our soul to Catholic Rome, guardian of the Catholic Faith and the traditions necessary to maintain it, and to Eternal Rome, mistress of wisdom and truth.

"On the other hand we refuse and have always refused to follow the Rome of the neo-Modernist and the new Protestant trend which was clearly evident in the Second Vatican Council and, after the Council in all the reforms which flowed from it."

The words were no doubt rather sharp but they expressed and still express my thinking. It was on account of this text that the Commission of Cardinals decided to bring about our downfall, because they could not do so on account of the way the seminary was run. The Cardinals were to tell me two months later that the Apostolic Visitors had gained a good impression from their inquiry.

On the following 13th February I was invited (by the Commission) to a "discussion" in Rome to clarify certain points and I went there without suspecting that it was a trap. The discussion turned itself from the start into a close cross-examination of a judicial type. It was followed by a second on the 3rd March and two months later the Commission informed me, "with the complete approval of His Holiness," of the decisions it had taken: Mgr. Mamie, the new Bishop of Fribourg, was accorded the right to withdraw the approval given to the Fraternity by his predecessor. Thereby the Fraternity and also the foundations, notably the Seminary of Ecône, lost the "right to exist."

Without waiting for notification of these decisions, Mgr. Mamie wrote to me: "I hereby inform you that I withdraw the acts and concessions effected by my predecessor with regard to the Priestly Fraternity of St. Pius X, in particular the decree of foundation dated the 1st November 1970. This decision takes effect immediately."

If you have followed me closely, you will be able to see that this suppression was made by the Bishop of Fribourg and not by the Holy See. By virtue of Canon 493, it is therefore completely void in law for lack of competence. Added to that there is a lack of sufficient cause. The decision can only be based on my declaration of the 21st November

1974, judged by the Commission to be "unacceptable on all points," because of the Commission's own admission the results of the Apostolic Visitation were favorable. Yet my declaration has never been the subject of a condemnation by the Congregation for the Doctrine of the Faith (the former Holy Office) which alone is competent to judge whether it is opposed to the Catholic Faith. It has only been deemed "unacceptable on all points" by three cardinals in the course of what remains officially a discussion.

The juridical existence of the Commission itself has never been proved. By what pontifical act was it instituted? On what date? What form did it take? Who was notified of it? The fact that the Roman authorities refuse to produce any such act permits us to doubt its existence. If there is doubt about its validity a law is not binding, says the Code of Canon Law. Even less so when there is doubt about the competence or even the existence of the authority. The words "with the complete approval of His Holiness" are not legally sufficient; they cannot take the place of the decree which should have constituted the Commission of Cardinals and defined its powers.

There are procedural irregularities which render the suppression of the Fraternity a nullity. Nor must we forget that the Church is not a totalitarian society of the Nazi or Marxist type, and that the law even when it is properly observed—which was not the case in this instance—is not an absolute. It has to be related to faith, truth and life. Canon Law is designed to make us live spiritually and thus to lead us to Eternal Life. If this law is used to prevent us from attaining it, or as it were to abort our spiritual life, we are obliged to disobey exactly in the same way that citizens are obliged to disobey the abortion laws of the State.

To return to the juridical aspect, I entered two successive appeals before the Apostolic Signatura, which is more or less the equivalent of a court of appeal in civil law. The Cardinal Secretary of State, Mgr. Villot, forbade this supreme tribunal of the Church to entertain them, which amounts to an interference by the executive in the judiciary.

XX
The Mass of All Time

One fact cannot have failed to surprise you: at no time during this affair has the Mass been in issue, although it is at the heart of the conflict. This enforced silence is the tacit admission that what is called the Rite of St. Pius V remains fully authorized.

On this subject Catholics can be perfectly easy in their minds: this Mass is not forbidden and cannot be forbidden. St. Pius V who, let us repeat, did not invent it but "re-established the Missal in conformity with the ancient rule and the rites of the Holy Fathers," gives us every guarantee in the Bull *Quo Primum*, signed by him on the 14th July 1570: "We have decided and declare that the Superiors, Canons, Chaplains and other priests by whatever title they are known, or Religious of whatsoever Order, may not be obliged to celebrate Mass otherwise than as enjoyed by Us. We likewise order and declare that no-one whosoever shall ever at any time be forced or coerced into altering this Missal: and this present Constitution can never be revoked or modified, but shall for ever remain valid and have the force of law . . . Should anyone venture to (make such an alteration), let him understand that he will incur the wrath of Almighty God and of the Blessed Apostles Peter and Paul."

Supposing that the Pope could withdraw this perpetual indult, he would have to do it by an equally solemn act. The Apostolic Constitution *Missale Romanum* of the 3rd April 1969 authorizes the so-called Mass of Paul VI, but contains no expressly formulated prohibition of the Tridentine Mass.[15] So much so that Cardinal Ottaviani could say in 1971: "The Tridentine Rite has not been abolished as far as I know." Bishop Adam, who claimed at the Plenary Assembly of the Swiss Bishops that the Constitution *Missale Romanun* had forbidden the celebration of the Rite of St. Pius V except by indult, had to retract when he was asked to say in what terms this prohibition had been declared.

It follows from this that if a priest were censured or even excommunicated on this ground, the sentence would be absolutely invalid. St. Pius V has canonized this Holy Mass, and a Pope cannot remove such a canonization any more than he can revoke that of a saint. We can celebrate it and the faithful can attend it with complete peace of mind, knowing furthermore it is the best way of maintaining their faith.

This is so much the case that His Holiness John Paul II, after several years of silence on the subject of the Mass, has finally loosened the fetter imposed on Catholics. The letter of the Congregation for Divine Worship, dated the 3rd October 1984, "authorizes" anew the Rite of St. Pius V for the faithful who request it. It imposes, admittedly, conditions we cannot accept, and in any case we did not need this indult to enjoy a right which has been granted to us until the end of time.

However, this initial gesture—let us pray that there will be others—lifts the suspicion unjustly cast on the Mass and liberates the consciences of those confused Catholics who still hesitate to attend it.

Let us now come to the suspension *a divinis* laid on me on the 22nd July 1976. It followed the ordinations of the 29th June at Ecône; for three months we had been receiving from Rome reproofs, supplications, orders and threats to persuade us to cease our activity and not to proceed to the priestly ordinations. Over the last few days beforehand

---

15. Tridentine, referring to the Council of Trent.

there was no end to the messages and deputations, and what were they saying? Six times they asked me to re-establish normal relations with the Holy See by accepting the new rite and celebrating it myself. They went to the length of sending a Monsignor who offered to concelebrate with me and they put a new missal in my hand with the promise that, if I said the Mass of Paul VI on the 29th June in front of all the people who had come to pray for the new priests, everything would thenceforth be smoothed out between Rome and myself.

This means that they were not prohibiting me from performing these ordinations, but they wanted it done according to the new liturgy. It was clear from that moment that the whole drama between Rome and Ecône was being played around the problem of the Mass, and it still is today.

I said, in the sermon of the Ordination Mass: "Tomorrow perhaps our condemnation will appear in the newspapers; it is very possible as a result of today's ordinations. I will probably have a suspension laid on me and these young priests will be stamped with an irregularity which ought theoretically to prevent them from saying Holy Mass. It is possible. Well, I appeal to St. Pius V."

Certain Catholics may have been troubled by my disregard of this suspension *a divinis*. But what must be fully understood is that it all forms a chain of events. Why was I forbidden to perform these ordinations? Because the Fraternity was suppressed and the seminary was supposed to have been closed. But I had not accepted the suppression and the closure, precisely because they had been illegally decided and the measures taken were tainted with various canonical defects, both of form and substance (notably what writers on administrative law call "misapplication of powers," that is to say the employment of powers against the purpose for which they should be used). To accept the suspension I would have to accept everything from the beginning; but I did not because we had been condemned without trial, without the opportunity to defend ourselves, without due warning or written process and without appeal.

Once one rejects the first judgment there is no reason not to reject the others, because the others depend on it. The nullity of one entails the nullity of those which follow.

Another question is sometimes put to the faithful and to priests: can you be in the right against everybody else? At a press conference, the representative of *Le Monde* said to me: "But after all, you are on your own. On your own against the Pope and all the bishops. What sense is there in your struggle?" Well, no, I am not alone. I have the whole of Tradition with me and the Church exists in time and space. Besides, I know that many bishops think like us in their hearts. Today, since the open letter to the Pope which Bishop Castro Mayer signed with me, there are two of us who have declared ourselves openly against the protestantization of the Church. We have many priests with us. Then there are our seminaries which now provide around 40 new priests each year, our 250 seminarians, our 30 brothers, our 60 nuns, our 30 oblates, the monasteries and Carmels which are opening and developing, and the crowds of the faithful who are coming to us.

Besides, the Truth does not depend on numbers and numbers do not make the Truth. Even if I were alone and all my seminarians left me, even if the whole of public opinion were to abandon me, that would be a matter of indifference as far as I am concerned. I am bound to my Creed, to my catechism, to the Tradition which has sanctified the Elect in Heaven and I want to save my soul. We know public opinion all too well. It condemned Our Lord a few days after having acclaimed Him. It is Palm Sunday followed by Good Friday. His Holiness Paul VI asked me: "But after all, don't you feel in your heart something that reproaches you for what you are doing? You are causing in the Church an enormous scandal, enormous. Doesn't your conscience tell you so?"

I replied: "No, Holy Father, not at all." If I had something to reproach myself with, I would stop at once.

Pope John Paul II has neither confirmed nor quashed the sanction pronounced against me. During the audience which he granted me in November 1979, he seemed after a long conversation quite disposed to allow freedom of choice in the liturgy, in short to let me do what I asked from the beginning, to carry on the "Experiment of Tradition" among all the other experiments that are carried on in the Church. The moment had come when perhaps everything could have been settled; no more outlawing of the Mass and no more problems. But Cardinal Seper, who was present, saw the danger.

"But, Holy Father," he exclaimed, "they make this Mass into a banner!"

The heavy curtain which had lifted for a moment fell back. We must still wait.

XXI
Neither a Heretic Nor a Schismatic

My statement of 21 November 1974, which triggered off the proceedings of which I have spoken, ended with these words: "In doing so . . . we are convinced of remaining loyal to the Catholic and Roman Church and to all the successors of Peter, and of being faithful dispensers of the Mysteries of Our Lord Jesus Christ." When publishing the text, the *Osservatore Romano* omitted this paragraph. For ten years and more our opponents have been set on casting us out of the Church's communion by presenting us as not accepting the Pope's authority. It would be very convenient to turn us into a sect and declare us schismatics. How many times the word schism has been applied to us!

I have not ceased repeating that if anyone separates himself from the Pope, it will not be I. The question comes down to this: the power of the Pope within the Church is supreme, but not absolute and limitless, because it is subordinate to the Divine authority which is expressed in Tradition, Holy Scripture, and the definitions already promulgated by the Church's magisterium. In fact, the limits of papal power are set by the ends for which it was given to Christ's Vicar on earth, ends which Pius IX clearly defined in the Constitution *Pastor aeternus* of the First Vatican Council. So in saying this I am not expressing a personal theory.

Blind obedience is not Catholic; nobody is exempt from responsibility for having obeyed man rather than God if he accepts orders from a higher authority, even the Pope, when these are contrary to the Will of God as it is known with certainty from Tradition. It is true that one cannot envisage such an eventuality when the Papal infallibility is engaged; but this happens only in a limited number of cases. It is an error to think that every word uttered by the Pope is infallible.

Nevertheless, I am not among those who insist or insinuate that Paul VI was a heretic and therefore, by that very fact, no longer Pope. John Paul I and John Paul II would then not have been legitimately elected. This is the position of those called "sede-vacantists."

It has to be admitted that Paul VI has posed a serious problem for the consciences of the faithful. This pontiff has done more harm to the Church than the French Revolution. There are definite acts of his, such as his signature to Article 7 of the *Institutio Generalis* of the new Mass, and likewise to the Council's document on Religious Liberty, that are scandalous. But it is not a simple problem to know whether a Pope can be a heretic. A good many theologians think he can be as a private teacher but not as a teacher of the Universal Church. We have to consider the degree to which the Pope intended to involve his infallibility in cases such as those I have quoted.

Now, we have already been able to perceive that he behaved more like a liberal than as one attached to heresy. In fact, as soon as the danger he risked was brought to his attention, he rendered the text contradictory by adding a formula meaning the contrary of what was already in the draft. A well-known example is the explanatory foreword to the Council's Constitution *Lumen Gentium* on collegiality.

Paul VI's liberalism, recognized by his friend Cardinal Daniélou, is sufficient to explain the disasters of his pontificate. The liberal Catholic is two-sided; he is in a state of continual contradiction. He would like to remain a Catholic but he is possessed by a desire to please the world. Can a Pope be a liberal and still remain a Pope? The Church has always severely reprimanded liberal Catholics, but has not always excommunicated them. Another argument put forward by the sede-vacantists is that the exclusion of Cardinals of eighty years and over, and the secret meetings which preceded and organized the last two conclaves render the election of those two Popes invalid. To assert that they were invalid is going too far; doubtful, perhaps. Nevertheless, the subsequent unanimous acceptance of the elections by the Cardinals and the Roman clergy sufficies to validate them. That is the opinion of theologians.

The reasoning of those who deny that we have a Pope puts the Church in an inextricable situation. The visibility of the Church is too necessary for its existence for it to be possible that God would allow it to disappear for decades. Who would be able to tell us where the future Pope is? How can he be elected if there are no more Cardinals? We detect a schismatic spirit behind those reasonings, and our Society utterly refuses to follow them. While rejecting Paul VI's liberalism, we wish to remain attached to Rome and the Successor of St. Peter out of fidelity to his predecessors.

It is obvious that in matters such as religious liberty, eucharistic hospitality as authorized by the new Canon Law, and collegiality considered as the affirmation of two supreme powers within the Church, it is the duty of every priest and every faithful Catholic to refuse obedience. This resistence must be made public if the evil is public and constitutes a cause of scandal for souls. This is the reason why, taking our line from St. Thomas Aquinas, Bishop de Castro Mayer and I on 21st November 1983 sent an open letter to Pope John Paul II begging him to denounce the principal causes of the dire situation which is dividing the Church. All the steps we have taken in private during the last fifteen years had proved unavailing; yet to remain silent would have seemed to make us accomplices in the unsettling of the faithful that is a fact throughout the world.

"Most Holy Father," we wrote, "it is an urgent matter that this unrest be quieted, because the flock have scattered and the abandoned sheep are following hirelings. We urge you, for the well-being of the Catholic faith and the salvation of souls, to re-affirm the truths contrary to these errors." Our cry of alarm was rendered even more urgent by the errors in the new Code of Canon Law, not to say its heresies, and by the ceremonies and speeches marking the fifth centenary of the birth of Martin Luther.

We have had no reply, but we have done what we ought to do. We must not despair as though it were a human undertaking. The present convulsion will pass away just as all heresies have passed away. One day a return will have to be made to Tradition: in the Papal authority the powers signified by the tiara must again re-appear; a tribunal for the protection of the truths of faith and morals must be restored permanently, and bishops must regain their powers and their personal initiative.

True apostolic work will have to be freed of all the impediments that now are paralyzing it by obscuring the essentials of the message. Seminaries must be brought back to their true function, religious orders revived, Catholic schools and universities restored by freeing them of secular State curricula. Support must be given to employers' and workers' organizations determined to collaborate in a fraternal manner, respecting the duties and rights of all, and renouncing that social scourge the strike, which is nothing better than a cold war within the nation. It will be necessary, too, to promote civil legislation that is in harmony with the laws of the Church, and to encourage the putting forward of Catholics for public office, who are actuated by the will to guide society towards the official recognition of the social rule of Christ the King.

For, after all, what do we say each day when we pray? "Thy kingdom come, Thy will be done, on earth as it is in heaven." And in the *Gloria* of the Mass? "Thou alone art the Lord, Jesus Christ." We sing that, but as soon as we get outside we say, "Oh no, these ideas are out of date: impossible to think of talking about the Kingdom of Christ in the world of today." We are living a contradiction. Are we Christians or not?

Nations are struggling with insoluble difficulties. There is endless war in many areas, and all mankind trembles in contemplating the possibility of a nuclear catastrophe. Solutions are sought that will restore the economy, stabilize

money, eliminate unemployment, and make industry prosperous. Well, even from the economic point of view, it is
necessary that Christ should reign, because that means the
reign of love and of the commandments of God, which ensure a balance in society and bring justice and peace. Is it a
Christian attitude to set one's hopes on this or that politician, or combination of parties, in the hope that eventually
one program or another will definitely and finally solve our
problems, when the one and only Lord is deliberately excluded as if He had nothing to do with human affairs?
What sort of a faith have people who live their lives in two
compartments with a rigid barrier separating their religion
from all their political, professional and other preoccupations? Is not God, who created heaven and earth, able to
solve our wretched material and social problems? If you
have ever prayed yourself in difficult moments of your life,
you will know by experience that He does not give stones
when His children ask Him for bread.

The Christian social order is at the opposite pole to the
Marxist ideas which, in whatever part of the world they
have been applied, have never brought anything but misery, oppression of the weakest, contempt for man, and
death. Christian social order respects private property, protects the family against corrupting influences, and encourages large families and the presence of the mother in the
home. It allows private enterprise a proper independence,
and encourages medium and small businesses. It is in favor
of a return to the land and appreciates agriculture as its
true value. It supports professional associations, freedom of
education, and the protection of the citizens against every
form of subversion and revolution.

This Christian order is quite different also from those
liberal systems based on the separation of Church and State,
whose powerlessness to overcome crises becomes increasingly obvious. How could it be otherwise when they have
deliberately cut themselves off from Him who is "the light
of men?" How could they muster the energies of their citizens when they have no ideal to put to them beyond pros

perity and comfort? They have been able to maintain an illusion for some time because the people have retained Christian habits of thinking and their rulers have more or less consciously kept some values. But at a time when everything is being questioned, these implicit references to the Will of God fade away. Liberal systems, when they are left to themselves and are no longer motivated by any higher idea, become exhausted and fall an easy prey to subversive ideologies.

To speak, then, of the Christian social order is not to cling to an out-moded past. On the contrary, it is a standpoint for the future which you should not hesitate to adopt. You are not fighting a rear-guard action; you are among those who know what's what because they take their lessons from Him who said, "I am the Way, the Truth and the Life." We have the advantage of possessing the truth. It is not our doing, we must not be conceited about it; but we must act accordingly. The possession of the truth is the advantage the Church has over error. It is up to her, helped by the grace of God, to spread it, and not timidly hide it under a bushel.

Still less should it be mingled with falsity, though this is what we are constantly witnessing. I read in *L'Osservatore Romano* (January 18, 1984) an interesting article by Paolo Befani about the favor shown to socialism by the Vatican. The author compares the situation in South America and that in Poland, and he writes:

"Leaving aside the situation in Europe, the Church finds herself confronted on the one hand by the situation in the Latin American countries and the influence over them of the U.S.A., and on the other hand by the situation of Poland in the orbit of the Soviet empire. Faced with these two frontiers the Church, which in Vatican II accepted and surpassed the liberal-democratic conquests of the French Revolution, and in her forward march proposes herself as the post-revolution to the Russian Marxist revolution, now offers a solution to the failure of Marxism of which the key idea is a post-Marxist, democratic, Christian-based, self-governing and non-totalitarian socialism.

"The Church's answer to the East is represented by Solidarity, raising the Cross in front of the Lenin ship-yards. Latin America's mistake is to seek the solution in Marxist communism, that is, in a socialism with anti-Christian roots."

There we have a fine example of liberal illusions, associating contradictory words in the conviction of expressing the truth! It is to these adulterous dreamers obsessed with the idea of marrying the Church to the Revolution that we owe the present chaos in the Christian world which is opening the doors to Communism. Saint Pius X said of the Sillonists, "they hanker for socialism, their eyes fixed on a chimera." Their successors are continuing to do so. After Christian Democracy comes Christian Socialism. We shall end up with Christian Atheism!

The solution that we seek must bring the answer not only to the failure of Marxism but also to the failure of Christian Democracy, which no longer needs proof. There has been more than enough of compromise and of unnatural unions. What is it we are fishing for in these muddy waters? The Catholic holds the real key-idea; and his duty is to work with all his might, either personally in politics or by his vote, to provide his country with representatives, both at the local and at the national level, who are resolved to re-establish a Christian social order, such as is alone capable of bringing peace, justice and true liberty. There is no other solution.

XXII
What Families Can Do

It is high time to react. When *Gaudium et Spes* speaks of the movement of history "becoming so rapid that everybody finds it hard to follow," we can take this as meaning the headlong rush of liberal society into disaggregation and chaos. We must take care not to follow!

One cannot understand how the leaders can claim to be of the Christian religion whilst destroying all authority within the State. On the contrary, it is important to re-establish this authority which is prescribed by Providence in the two natural societies of divine right, the family and civil society, whose influence here below is fundamental. In recent times it is the family that has suffered the hardest blows. The changeover to Socialism in countries like France and Spain has only speeded up the process.

The ensuing legal measures demonstrate a great cohesion in their determination to ruin the institution of the family; the reducing of parental authority, easy divorce, the disappearance of responsibility in the procreative act, the legal recognition of irregular unions and even of homosexual couples, juvenile cohabitation, trial marriage, the reduction of financial and social assistance to large families, etc... The State itself in its own interests is beginning to see the effects of this in the declining birth rate, and wonders how in the near future the rising generations will be able to maintain the pensions of those who are no longer economically active. But the effects are considerably more serious in the spiritual field.

Catholics must not follow, but as citizens they must

bring all their weight to bear to put right what is needed. This is why they may not remain aloof from politics. However, their endeavors will be most effective in the upbringing they give their children.

On the subject, authority is contested at its very source by those who declare, "Parents are not the owners of their children," by which they mean that their education reverts to the State with its schools, its day nurseries and its kindergarten schools. They reproach parents with failing to respect the "freedom of conscience" of their children when they bring them up in accordance with their own religious convictions.

These ideas can be traced back to the seventeenth-century English philosophers who maintained that men are separate individuals, independent from birth, all equal and free from all authority. We know that to be false. The child receives everything from his father and his mother, all nourishment—bodily, intellectual, educational, moral and social. Parents are aided in this by teachers who in the children's minds share their authority, but whether it be from either or both of them, almost all the learning they obtain during their youth will be received and accepted, rather than gathered by observation and personal experience. A considerable part of knowledge comes from the authority who passes it on. The pupil has confidence in his parents, in his teachers and in his books and thereby his knowledge grows.

This is even more true of religious knowledge, of religious practice, of moral training in conformity with the faith, with tradition, and customs. Men generally live by following family traditions, as can be observed throughout the whole world. Conversion to another religion from that received during childhood presents serious difficulties.

This extraordinary influence of the family and background was intended by God. He willed that His blessings should first of all be passed on by the family. This is the reason why He gives to the father of a family such great authority and power over his family, his wife and his children. A child is born in such extreme weakness that we can appreciate the absolute need for the stability and indissolubility of the home.

To want to exalt a child's personality and consciousness to the detriment of parental authority is ruinous for him, driving him to revolt and to despise his parents, whereas long life is promised to those who honor their parents. Saint Paul, in reminding us of this, makes it a duty for fathers not to exasperate their sons, but to bring them up in the discipline and fear of the Lord.

If we had to wait to receive an understanding of religious truth before believing and conversion, there would be very few Christians today. We believe the truths of religion because its witnesses are worthy of belief by their holiness, their unselfishness and their charity. As Saint Augustine says, faith gives understanding.

The role of parents has become very difficult. As we have seen, the majority of Catholic schools have in effect become secular. The true religion is no longer taught in them, nor yet the natural sciences in the light of the faith. The catechisms spread Modernism. The hectic style of modern living leaves no spare time and professional obligations separate parents and children from the grandfathers and grandmothers who before used to help with their upbringing. Catholics are now not only confused but also defenseless.

Not to such an extent, however, that they cannot provide the essentials, the grace of God making up what lacks. What must be done? Truly Catholic schools do exist, though few in number. Send your children to them even if it is a financial burden. Open new schools, as others have already done. If you are only able to use schools where the teaching has been distorted, then you must complain and demonstrate against it; do not allow the teachers to cause your children to lose their faith.

Read and re-read as a family the Catechism of Trent, the finest, the soundest and the most complete. Organize "parallel catechism classes" under the spiritual direction of good priests, do not be afraid of being called, like us, "rebel." Moreover, there are already numerous groups operating who would welcome your children.

Throw out the books that carry Modernist poison. Seek advice. There are courageous publishers printing excellent works and re-printing those destroyed by the Modernists. Do not buy just any Bible; every Catholic family ought to have a faithful translation of the Vulgate, the Latin version made by Saint Jerome in the fourth century and canonized by the Church.

Hold on to the true interpretation of the Scriptures, keep to the true Mass and the Sacraments such as were formerly administered everywhere. At the present time the devil is assailing the Church: that is the fact of the matter. We are witnessing perhaps one of his last battles, an all-out battle. He is attacking on all fronts; and if Our Lady of Fatima said that one day he would penetrate to the highest positions of the Church, we must believe that could happen. Personally, I am alleging nothing, yet there are signs which could make us think that in the highest administrative bodies in Rome there are men who have lost their faith.

Urgent spiritual remedies must be applied. We must pray and do penance, as the Blessed Virgin has requested, and say the Rosary together in the family. As we have seen during each war, people begin to pray together when the bombs begin to fall. In exactly the same way, they are falling at this moment; we are on the brink of losing faith. Do you realize that that would surpass in seriousness every catastrophe feared by man, such as world economic crisis or atomic warfare?

Renewal is absolutely necessary; but you must not assume that you cannot count on the young for that. The whole of youth is not corrupted, as some try to convince us. Many of them hold an ideal; for many others it would be enough to offer them one. There are boundless examples of movements that have successfully appealed to their generosity; those monasteries faithful to Tradition are drawing them, and there is no lack of vocations from young seminarists or novices wanting to be accepted. There is a magnificent undertaking to be accomplished in conformity with the instructions given by the Apostles, *"Tenete traditiones. Permanete in iis quae didicistis."* *"Keep the traditions. Stand fast in those things which you have learned"* (II Thessalonions 2:14).

The old world called upon to disappear is the world of abortion. Families who are faithful to Tradition are also large families and their very faith ensures their posterity. "Increase and multiply!" By keeping to what the Church has always taught you will ensure the future.

XXIII
Building Up Versus Pulling Down

Twenty years have gone by and one would have thought that the reactions raised by the Council reforms would have calmed down, that the Catholic people would have buried the religion in which they had been brought up, that the younger ones, not having known it, would have accepted the new one. That, at least, was the wager made by the Modernists. They were not unduly disturbed by the uproar, sure of themselves as they were in the early days. They were less so later on. The frequent and necessary concessions made to the spirit of the world did not produce the expected results. Nobody any longer wanted to be a priest of the new religion and the faithful turned away from their religious practice. The Church which tried to become a Church of the poor became a poor Church, obliged to resort to advertising to collect Peter's Pence, and to sell off its properties.

During this time those faithful to Tradition drew together in all the Christian lands, and particularly in France, Switzerland, the United States and Latin America.

The fabricator of the new Mass, Mgr. Annibale Bugnini was himself obliged to recognize this world-wide resistance in his posthumous book,[16] a resistance which is growing and organizing itself unceasingly and drawing support. No, the "traditionalist" movement is not "slowing-down" as the

16. *La Riforma Liturgica:* Edizioni Liturgiche Rome.

progressivist journalists write from time to time to reassure themselves. Where else are there as many people at Mass as at St. Nicholas-du-Chardonnet, and also as many Masses, as many Benedictions of the Blessed Sacrament or as many beautiful ceremonies? The Society of Saint Pius X throughout the world owns seventy houses, each with at least one priest, churches like the one in Brussels and the one we have quite recently bought in London, or the one placed at our disposal in Marseilles; also schools, and four seminaries.

Carmelite convents are opening and already forming new communities. Religious communities of men and of women created fifteen or more years ago, who strictly apply the rule of the orders from which they stem, are overflowing with vocations, and are continuously having to enlarge their premises and construct more buildings. The generosity of the Catholic faithful never ceases to amaze me, particularly in France.

The monasteries are centers of attraction, crowds of people go there often from far away; young people bewildered by the illusory seductions of pleasure and escape in every form, find in them their Road to Damascus. Here is a list of places where they have kept the true Catholic faith and for that reason draw people: Le Barroux, Flavigny-sur-Ozerain, La Haye-aux-Bonshommes, the Benedictines of Alés, the Sisters of Fanjeaux, of Brignolles, of Pontcallec, and communities like that of Father Lecareux . . .

Travelling a great deal, I see everywhere at work the hand of Christ blessing His Church. In Mexico the ordinary people drove from the churches the reforming clergy who, won over by the so-called liberation theology, wanted to throw out the statues of the saints. "It's not the statues who are going, it's you." Political circumstances have prevented us from opening a priory in Mexico; so faithful priests travel out from a center at El Paso near the frontier in the United States. The descendants of the *Cristeros* welcome them warmly and offer them their churches. I have administered 2500 confirmations there at the request of the people.

In the United States, young married couples with their numerous children flock to the Society's priests. In 1982 in that country I ordained the first three priests trained entirely in our seminaries. Groups of traditionalists are on the increase whereas the parishes are declining. Ireland, which has remained refractory towards the novelties, has been subject to the reforms since 1980, altars having been cast into rivers or re-used as building material. Simultaneously, traditionalist groups have formed in Dublin and Belfast. In Brazil, in the diocese of Campos of which I have already spoken, the people have rallied around the priests evicted from their parishes by the new bishop, with processions of 5,000 and 10,000 people taking to the streets.

It is therefore the right road we are following; the proof is there, we recognize the tree by its fruits. What the clergy and the laity have achieved in spite of persecution by the liberal clergy (for, as Louis Veuillot says, "There is nobody more sectarian than a liberal.") is almost miraculous. Do not let yourself be taken in, dear reader, by the term "traditionalist" which they would have people understand in a bad sense. In a way, it is a pleonasm because I cannot see who can be a Catholic without being a traditionalist. I think I have amply demonstrated in this book that the Church is a tradition. We are a tradition. They also speak of "integrism." If by that we mean respect for the integrality of dogma, of the catechism, of Christian morality, of the Holy Sacrifice of the Mass, then yes, we are integrists. And I do not see how one can be a Catholic without being an integrist in that sense of the word.

It has also been said that after me, my work will disappear because there will be no bishop to replace me. I am certain of the contrary; I have no worries on that account. I may die tomorrow, but the good Lord answers all problems. Enough bishops will be found in the world to ordain our seminarians: this I know.

Even if at the moment He is keeping quiet, one or another of these bishops will receive from the Holy Ghost the courage needed to arise in his turn. If my work is of God, He will guard it and use it for the good of the Church. Our Lord has promised us, the gates of Hell shall not prevail against her.

This is why I persist, and if you wish to know the real reason for my persistence, it is this. At the hour of my death, when Our Lord asks me: "What have you done with your episcopate, what have you done with your episcopal and priestly grace?" I do not want to hear from His lips the terrible words "You have helped to destroy the Church along with the rest of them."